Behold

the

Dreamer Cometh

&

Other Sermons

Neville Goddard

Contents

Contents

Behold *the* Dreamer Cometh

n the 37th chapter of Genesis we read the story of Joseph, a dreamer whose dreams always came true. His father, Israel, loved Joseph more than any of his other sons, and made him a long robe with sleeves. Now I ask you, who is Joseph? He is the foreshadowing of Jesus Christ, your true identity. Historical evidence for Jesus, the man, is nonexistent, yet he is the only reality and the true identity of every child born of woman. When you say within yourself, "I am," that is Jesus Christ, he who is dreaming this whole vast world into being.

One day you will understand this truth, for:

> *"Real are the dreams of gods*
> *And smoothly pass their pleasure*
> *In the long, immortal dream."*

Your thoughts are your dreams, which weave your world into being and sustain it. You and I are inserted into the dream. "'Tis we who, lost in stormy visions fight with phantoms, an unprofitable strife." And we will continue the dream until we awaken to discover that we are the dreamer, who is God himself.

This is not an idle dream, but one designed for the divine purpose of extending imagination's creative power. Expanding by entering his dream, God appears as you and I. And he is going to awaken from his dream, and, because there is only God, although we number into the billions we will all be resolved into the one Lord God Jehovah, who is Jesus Christ.

Now, Joseph could dream and interpret the dreams of others, regardless of their complexities. Certain dreams are simple and need no interpretation, but most of our dreams are symbolic and few

5

understand the language of symbolism. Joseph understood and interpreted the dream of the sheaves as well as his dream of the sun, the moon and eleven stars bowing before him. When his father heard the dream he said, "What is this dream? Shall I and your mother and brothers bow down to you?" He didn't criticize him, but set these things in his heart.

Now, in the state of Moses the name Joseph is changed to Joshua, which is the Hebraic form of the Anglicized word, "Jesus", or "Jehovah saves." So here we find Joseph the dreamer, becoming Jesus the savior, by awakening from the dream he dreamed, interpreted, and fulfilled.

Right now, you think this room is real, and tonight you might have a dream and - if you are lucky - remember it as a dream, but not as reality. Well, if to dream is to dwell in unreality not knowing it as such, what is life but one uninterrupted dream? Until you have certain experiences, you will no doubt question my sanity, but when you have them you will know that this which seems real is no less a dream than the dream of the night.

Travel with me in your mind as we read the morning paper. On the first page we read of an air crash, a war, a hold-up, a murder, and embezzlement. Turn the page to the social column. See the pictures of the bride and groom and read all about their wedding and the guests attending. Another page lists the deaths, and finally we turn to the financial page, which tells us who is making money and who is losing it. Isn't that disjointed? Lost in the reading, we have traveled from violence to a wedding, to gossip, deaths, and finance. All written by ten or twelve men who are sound asleep, and dreaming their columns into being, while you - and the millions who read the paper - will see the outpicturing of all that you thought during the reading.

How do I know this? Because I have awakened from the dream of life. I know that God laid himself down within me to sleep, to dream that he is I; for when he awoke, I was he! How do I know that I am he? Because his only begotten son, David, called me father.

While I remain in this body of blood and flesh, I must abide by its restrictions and limitations; yet remembering it is a dream, I can change it. If this world is reality I cannot change it; but if I am its reality, I can change my world relative to myself. I can imagine a desire fulfilled and watch it come to pass in my outer world. But first I had to know it was a dream. This I do know, for he who is in the depth of my own being said to me: "I laid myself down within you to sleep and as I slept I dreamed a dream. I dreamed that I am you." Yes, he dreamed that he is I, for he awoke and he was I. A few months later he revealed his mystery to me by bringing his son David to call me father. Through an innate wisdom I knew he wasn't just a boy who called me father, but the David of Biblical fame who is God's only son.

When God awakes within you he is the same God who awoke within me. There aren't two Gods. You and I are really one. Although there appears to be billions of us here, we are all one being, one God acting out this play, to expand our creative power and wisdom.

A very dear friend of mine is in the audience tonight. I am so thrilled for him and for anyone who comes and has such an experience and shares it with me. This is his experience. While in his living room watching TV he felt drowsy, closed his eyes, and allowed himself to fall asleep. Remembering he was watching TV, he finds himself driving his car with his wife at his side. Feeling a sense of impending disaster, as his wife grabbed the wheel he awoke in the dream, and succeeded in getting control of the wheel again. Up ahead he saw a man he recognized as a great actor, and suddenly remembering where he was when the dream began, he inwardly proclaimed I AM. At that moment he awoke seated on his chair facing the TV. Then he said, "Since this is the first time I awoke in a dream to know who I am and where I am, I can't help but be pleased with myself." Well, he should be. All of these experiences are little breakages to the brain that bind us to the dream, which means that he is on the verge of awakening from this dream of life.

Unnumbered times I have sat in my chair and found myself slipping into what reason tells me I should not see. I have stepped into that world; it closes around me and becomes just as real as this. I am in a terrestrial world, talking to people who are just as solid and real as you are and I am. Awake, I am aware of where I was when I entered this section of time. and I also know that there is no road to take me back to the year and place I left.

You see, all things are taking place now. Eternity exists and all things in eternity independent of creation, which was an act of mercy. Entering a certain section of the dream, we animate it and become aware of that which already is. The past has not ceased to be. It is taking place as it took place and still takes place when anyone enters that section of time. The same is true with the future. The year 1969 finds us standing on the moon. It always has been so. The world is, and we are placed upon this little space called earth to learn to bear the beams of love, for God is infinite love. I know, for I stood in His presence, then came down and entered a specter in order to learn to love and take on substance.

Not long ago I was in another section of time instructing a group of maybe a dozen men all seated around me. In the center with me was a spectrum, a shadow of a man. I could move him about and do with him as I willed. Then I said to him, "Go and love. To the degree that you love, you will acquire substance. Only then can you take part in the drama and awake with life in yourself."

What I said to those men I say to you now. At the present time you are only an animated being, not a life-giving spirit. One day you will acquire substance (acquire love) then you will become one with life in yourself, knowing that all things were made through the creative act of love (the act of mercy) and without it was not anything made. As life-giving spirits, we all return to the one being as that one being, yet retaining our own identity. We will never lose our identity, but rather we will grow ever-greater individualization.

While In San Francisco, a chap who attended my meetings there told me a story. One hot summer's day he stopped in a bar for a nice cold beer. Taking the only unoccupied seat at the bar, he was soon visiting with the man sitting next to him who told him this story.

"The strangest thing happened to me years ago and it haunts me still. I was wounded during the Korean War and shipped to a hospital in Japan. While lying on that bed in the hospital and knowing I am an American, I felt the room fade from my view and suddenly I am in Europe, dancing with a lady who is dressed, like all the other ladies there, in hoop skirts. Knowing who I am, I said to my dancing partner, 'You know, this is a dream,' and with that remark she became frightened. As people gathered around me I told them that I was really an American soldier who was wounded in a hospital in Japan. I even told them what year it was, but to them the year had not yet arrived so the crowd became angry and I decided it was time to leave. So, I simply assumed I was on my bed in the hospital in Japan, and when I opened my eyes, I was there."

This man hasn't yet completely awakened, but one day he will awaken from this dream that seems so consistent, just as you will. And when you do, you will experience every precept of scripture in what the world will call a dream.

Now, the 6th chapter of I Timothy tells us that "The love of money is the root of all evil," and in the 13th chapter of the epistle to the Hebrews, Paul tells us to: "Keep your life free from the love of money." When I was a little boy in the island of Barbados, every Sunday four of us boys would ride a big male donkey we used to sire horses to produce mules, down to my grandmother's house, where she would give each of us a coin. I received a penny. When we got out of my grandmother's sight, a man would meet us with a female donkey, and for my penny he would get on the back of his donkey and we would have wild ride home as our jackass chased his female donkey. This went on for a long time before my mother found out, and then she said: "You know, Nev, you aren't going to have anything, for you give everything away." I knew, intuitively, that the love of money was the root of all evil.

Now, to show how scripture fulfills itself in experience, I will share with you now a recent waking dream of mine. I knew where my physical body was, and I knew what year it was, but I found myself standing on a street corner holding an enormous packet of bills of all denominations. As a woman passed by she reached over and grabbed some of my money. In her eagerness, several bills floated away from her and were grabbed by the other people passing by. Suddenly this lady became very angry and demanded that they all give her money back to her! She had just stolen it from me, but was now accusing the others of stealing it from her! Isn't that life? A man can trace the ownership of his property back to his forefathers who stole it, but he would be as mad as can be if a relative of the original owner tried to reclaim his property.

Now, in my dream I kept on moving through the labyrinthine ways of my mind, objectifying what I am encountering. Suddenly a man approached and asked if I wanted a taxi. Still holding my money, I refused his invitation. Then many men began to gather around me and when I saw their faces, and their knives, I realized they were going to take my money as well as my life, so I reminded myself of where I was when I began the dream. I knew that if I awoke I would defeat their intention. I would survive, but none of us would get the money. The moment my decision was made, I dropped the money and returned to my bed. Now I know the truth of the statement, "The love of money is the root of all evil" for my vision is part of the eternal structure of the universe.

You, too, will have a vision such as mine after you have lost all desire for money. Yes, you will desire the necessary means to meet the needs of Caesar: to pay rent, taxes, and buy food and clothing; but you will know that you don't need a billion to meet them. Those who are hungry for more and more billions are sound asleep. If they heard what I am telling you now they would think me insane; but I would tell them that their dreams reveal a far deeper insanity, for they are sound asleep, believing their dreams to be reality.

Now, in the story, Jesus was a dreamer whose father so loved him he made him a robe with long sleeves. I wondered what was the importance of the sleeves, and then one night I had this experience. I was teaching the great mystery of God when a man entered the room and severed the sleeve of my robe to expose my right arm from the shoulder to my fingertips. The next morning, I turned to the Book of Isaiah and read, "Who will believe our report? To whom has the arm of the Lord been revealed?" That night the sleeve of the robe worn by Joseph the dreamer, was severed, revealing my arm - the symbol of my imaginative power.

I know, now, that I - all imaginative power - have awakened from the dream. I know that is what you are also. I am trying to convince you of this, and ask you to test yourselves. If this world is real, you can't change it, for you cannot change reality; but you can change a dream. Feel the changes have now come upon you. Immerse yourself in that feeling and sustain it. If this is a dream, that which you are feeling will produce objective facts for others to see as real. But you will remember its origin was a dream. Once it becomes objective and real, don't get lost in the dream, for like all dreams, it will fade away. Everything comes into being, waxes, wanes, and vanishes. A tree may be 8000 years old, but it will eventually die. The stars are melting away because they are the dreams of the gods and

"Real are the dreams of gods
And smoothly pass their pleasure
In a long, immortal dream."

Imagination (gods) brought the world into being and sustains it while this grand experiment is taking place. We are those gods (called sons) who collectively form God the Father.

No child is born that is not clothing a son of God, as told us in the 32nd chapter of the Book of Deuteronomy. "He has put bounds to the people according to the number of the sons of God." A child could not breathe without God's entrance as his breath. "God himself enters death's door, the human skull, and lays down in the grave of man in visions of eternity until he awakes and sees the linen clothes lying there that the females wove for him at the gate of his Father's house."

When I entered this garment that my mother - a female - wove for me, God - whose name is I AM - entered with me and began his dream.

My mother called me Neville, and as time went by, I began to claim that I am Neville. Then one day we became one new being, for the "I" who entered the garment named Neville awoke to discover I am God. Then to prove to myself that I truly am He, God's son appeared before me and called me Father. Now, restrained by the body that I wear, I am limited and weak. But when I take it off and the world calls me dead, I will return to the one being out of which I came, for I came out from the Father and came into the world. Again, I am leaving the world and returning to the Father.

If you know that you are God the Father, you will know that it does not matter what the world dreams. No matter how horrible the dream may appear to be, the dreamer is untouched by his dream. He who dreamed he was Stalin and murdered millions, is untouched by his dream and in the end will discover that all things work towards God's awakening.

The plea in the 44th Psalm "Rouse thyself, why sleepest thou O Lord. Awake. Do not cast us off forever," is directed to God, the God in everyone who is struggling to awaken. He is waking in my friend Bill, who had the experience of driving his car, knowing he was seated in his living room. These kinds of experiences break the threads that bind one to his dream, and as these threads begin to break he awakes within his own skull, for that is where the drama takes place.

Now in the story, when Joseph joined his brothers, they said to one another: "Let us kill him." But his brother, Judah pleaded for his life, saying: "No, he is our flesh and blood. Do not let his blood be upon us. Let us sell him into slavery." So, they stripped him of his robe and threw him into a pit. Then a caravan, on its way to Egypt carrying gold, incense, and myrrh (the same things the kings brought to the Christ child at his birth) agreed to buy him; and Joseph was taken into Egypt, where he rose to the power of Pharaoh. Joseph then saved civilization from starvation. And when the brothers were sorry for what they had done, Joseph said: "You meant evil against me, but God meant it for good." Then his name was changed from Joseph to Joshua, which means Jesus.

Remember, scripture unfolds within you. The dreamer in you has been thrown into a pit. Now, in the 40th Psalm (which is so often used in the New Testament concerning Jesus) the 2nd verse reads: "They raised me up from the pit, out of the miry bog and placed my feet upon the rock, making my steps secure." The word "mire" is defined as "spongy earth." Can you think of anything that better describes the human brain? And man is called the earth, for the word "Adam" means "red earth." So, the dreamer is taken out of the pit - the skull where he has been locked in - by awakening from his dream and being born from above.

You must experience two births: a physical one and a spiritual one. You are spiritually born through the awakening and resurrection of Jesus Christ from the dead. It is not another being born; you are he; for you are all alone, and when you leave your tomb is empty.

The New Testament is all about the dreamer in you who awakens as Jesus Christ, and everything said of him is true. His history is divine, not secular.

You will never find any evidence of an historical Christ here on earth. Bishop Pike went looking, yet never found who Christ really is. The Pope, as well as the leaders of all Christian religions, have millions of people looking to them as guides; yet they are all blind leaders of the blind. The historical evidence of Christ as a man is nonexistent, yet he is the only reality and the true identity of every child born of woman.

You are Jesus Christ, sleeping, dreaming horrible dreams mixed with lovely ones; but in the end you will awaken from the dream to know you are Jesus Christ. You will then remain a little while to tell your experiences to those who are willing to be disillusioned and will allow their false ideas of the past to fall away; then you will leave this little shadow that walks across the earth to enter eternity as God.

What I have told you will live in your minds. Hold fast to the visions I have shared with you, for in time my Word will take root and grow within you. Then this wonderful story will erupt in you, and you will know you, too, are Jesus Christ. And, because there is only one Jesus Christ and only one son, when God's son calls you Father, you and I are one. That is the fantastic mystery. How we, retaining our individuality, are one!

Now let us go into the silence.

Believe *in* Him

hen asked: "What must we do to be doing the work of God?" he answered: "Believe in him whom he has sent." That's all you have to do. Salvation is yours when you believe in him. There is no aristocracy of privilege, and to believe that Jesus exists means nothing. The question is: can you believe in his story?

He tells us he was sent, and everyone who is sent is Jesus, the sender. Those who are called from the world of death do not volunteer or choose the task. They are selected, called, incorporated into the body of the Risen Lord and sent as the sender, and can say: "He who sees me sees him who sent me." After incorporation into his being, the individual is sent - not to tell that he has a large family, a lovely home, or lots of money, but that he has fulfilled scripture.

When Jesus entered the synagogue he began to teach, and those who heard him wondered how he had such learning, since they knew he was only the carpenter's son. They knew his mother's name was Mary, his brothers' James, Jose, Simon, and Judas, as well as his sisters.

Here we see a large family, and a man with little or no learning teaching the scholars of the day. He tells them that he was sent - not to build a house or to tell others how to do it, but to fulfill scripture. Then, beginning with Moses and the law and all the prophets and the psalms, he interpreted to them in all the scriptures the things concerning himself. Not realizing that scripture was all about him, a normal man from a large family whose trade was that of a carpenter was called, incorporated into the Risen Man, and sent, knowing he was one with the one who sent him.

I can't divorce myself from the being that incorporated me into his body. He sent me to tell you that if you believe my experiences, you will also do the works that I do. If not, you will not do them, for there is no other way to salvation. Unless these mystical experiences unfold in you, you will never leave this world of death to live in the world of life.

In Adam all die. In Jesus all are made alive. He made me alive, in him, and sent me to tell you of my experiences - for the need was great - and to say that if you believe me, you will experience them and be saved, as they are your departure from this world of death and your entrance into the world of life.

I tell you: in spite of the fact that I have an earthly father and mother, brothers, and a sister, I am no longer of this world. I am from above and you are from below. If you will believe me, you, too, will be born from above. Then you will no longer be from below, but will be an entirely different being, living in an entirely different world.

Now, in the 16th chapter of Acts, we read the story of a slave girl who possessed the spirit of divination and was making a lot of money for her owners as a soothsayer. And when Paul came by with his associates, she said: "These men are proclaiming the way of salvation," and she followed them for many days. This story is followed by the imprisonment of Paul and a mighty earthquake, which awakened the jailer, who - trembling with fear - said: "What must I do to be saved?" And he was told to believe in the Lord Jesus.

To believe in a man? No. The Lord Jesus is only a pattern of salvation which is now encrusted with barnacles. I was called, incorporated into the body of love, and sent into the world to scrape off the barnacles by telling the path of salvation I have experienced.

You may think that the few hundred or thousand people I have told would mean nothing against three billion people in the world; but I know a remnant has been prepared, and they believe. That is all that is needed. Having heard, their belief causes it to happen in them; and salvation's story spreads once more, until those without vision organize and make a business out of it. Then it will once more grow barnacles and become a tradition, minus the spirit.

In 1929 I did not volunteer, but was called. I stood in the presence of Infinite Love, who incorporated me into his body. I was sent as love

- the body of the Risen Lord - back to a physical garment which is fragile, to tell those who are equally fragile that God is their own wonderful human imagination. Many, knowing my biological background, my large family with its limitations, reject my words. A few, however, have accepted them, and to that remnant it will happen.

So, what must you do to be doing the work of God? Believe in him whom He has sent. I tell you He has sent me. You may or may not believe me, that is your privilege. But I tell you: the experience so changed me that I have walked by faith in this vision through the mire of doubt, even when it came from my intimate circle.

One is first called, incorporated into the body of love, and then sent. This goes on eternally until all are redeemed, for not one will be lost. Just as by Adam all die, so also by Christ shall all be made alive. This Christ is a pattern of the eternal purpose of God, for there is only one way to escape this world.

The pattern begins by your birth as spirit. This is followed by the discovery of the fatherhood of God. Your spiritual body will be torn from top to bottom as you ascend into heaven. And the symbol of the Holy Spirit will descend upon you to smother you with love, completing the pattern.

Jesus Christ is not a man, but a pattern, which I have come to renew. To believe that Jesus Christ existed is not a belief in him, for he is the way to salvation!

Now, once the ship is encrusted with barnacles, one is called and sent to scrape them off by retelling the story as something that happened to him. When I told my family, they could not believe me and questioned me, saying: "Neville, you mean you do not believe in Jesus Christ?" And I replied: "I believe in him far more than you do!" "Don't you believe that he existed?" "Yes, but not as a man."

To believe in Jesus Christ, you believe in the pattern of salvation of which he is. If you believe in a man, you believe in Neville, and Neville means nothing. If Neville was called and incorporated into the spiritual pattern of salvation, he is sent bearing the pattern which erupts within him. This pattern has erupted in me and I have told my story as I was sent to do.

It is said that Jesus began his ministry when he was about thirty years of age. That doesn't mean thirty physical years, for he was not speaking as a biological man. Thirty years after he was incorporated into the body of love, he was qualified by the eruption to tell what had happened to him. He told his visions and pointed out their fulfillment of scripture, and some believed while others - so conditioned to believe in a physical Christ - could not understand.

The splitting of God's temple is told in its symbolic manner in the 14th chapter of Zechariah, as: "The Mount of Olives shall be split in two from east to west as one half moves north and the other half moves south leaving a very wide valley." It is told as a metaphor, but you are its reality. Scripture is all about you, and that splitting is yourself. Taken in a secular manner, David lived unnumbered years ago; but in the spirit, he will call you father.

When I share my visions and their scriptural confirmation, some believe me, but the majority think I am sharing a fantasy; yet I still walk with faith through the mire of doubt as I tell my story. My background is known. I have no education, no wealth or social position, yet I do know that I was chosen to be called and incorporated into the body of love and sent.

Love could have called a financial or intellectual giant, or someone handsome and wonderful, judged by human standards; yet he called me in the spirit. I was not initiated in the flesh, but was taken in spirit; for God is spirit, and those who worship him do so in spirit and in truth.

It was a spiritual incorporation into the body of love, yet it seemed to be solidly real. As Spirit, I returned to the garment I had left on the bed. It was that spiritual body which unfolded his plan of salvation. Now I know that this is the only way man can depart this world of death, and his departure begins by simply believing the story.

Don't believe in Neville as a man, for he is frail and subject to all of the weaknesses of the flesh. Rather, believe in what I have experienced. I have unfolded scripture for you and shown you where my experiences were foretold. I have repeated this over and over in the hope that those who hear my words will believe them, for I have tied the gospel to its reality.

The Book of Acts, once part of the Book of Luke, was detached for a purpose. The story of Jesus, the pattern man, is not found in the Book of Acts. Rather, the story of the apostles is recorded there; for the apostles are sent to tell exactly how it happened in them. I do not know, however, of any part of scripture where the story is told as graphically as I have told it to you.

In the Old Testament, the question is asked: "Can a man bear a child? Why then do I see every man with his hands pulling himself out of himself just like a woman in labor. Why does every face turn pale?" "To us a child is born; to us a son is given."

When a woman forms a child within herself, is that child not part of her body? And when she is in labor, does she not pull a part of her body out of herself? Primitive women did not go to a hospital. While working in the field, these women would stop for a moment and pull that which they had formed within themselves, out of themselves. This is exactly what I did. I pulled myself right out of myself.

Five months later I fulfilled the 89th Psalm. When David stood before me, I knew I was his father, as there was no uncertainty as to this relationship. I am telling you what I have experienced. Scripture foretold these visions, which must take place before you can depart this world. What must you do to bring them about? Believe in the story I have been sent to tell; for if you do, and set your hope fully upon having these experiences, your salvation is assured. Eventually everyone will believe. Rejection delays the birth, however, for it comes only after acceptance of the story told by the one who was sent.

I did not choose to be sent. When I fell asleep that night, I would have been the last person I would have chosen as worthy to be called into the presence of the Risen Lord. The Beatitudes tell us that only the pure in heart will see God, and I certainly did not feel myself to be pure in heart. My wife and I were separated, and my little boy was moving back and forth between us. With the conflicts which go with all these silly little things, I would never have judged myself worthy of being pure in heart.

But God does not see what man sees. God sees the heart. He sees the motive behind the act, never the outer picture. Was the thought brought forth in love, or to get even? Was its motive to inflict pain, or to express love? God sees the heart, and when He judges it as pure, that individual is called.

In 1929 I was called, and for thirty years I only taught the law. The promise was there in scripture, but I did not know it until it erupted in me thirty years later. From that moment on I could do nothing but think about it, talk about it, and share my experiences of it; for that is what I was sent to do.

My genealogy is known. My biological background - my father, mother, brothers, and sister, as well as my lack of education - is known; yet it is all recorded in scripture. When I shared my experiences with my family, they rejected them one hundred percent! My earthly father came the closest to understanding. One day a minister was at the house, and when he could not answer my questions, or throw any light upon my visions, my father said: "Son, you must be an apostle." My mother felt it in her womb when I was coming into this world; but she had no confirmation, as I became a dancer - and she had thought I would be a minister in the Anglican church.

But I tell you: this is the only way to salvation. Don't believe in Neville. He is not the way. I could go out with you every night and thoroughly enjoy matching you drink for drink. No food is distasteful to me, as I enjoy it all.

I am told I am not discriminating enough, for I can find nothing to condemn. I do, however, admit to all of my weaknesses of the human flesh; yet in spite of that I was called and sent. At the time I did not know God's purpose; but after his message erupted within me,

I knew I was sent to refresh the atmosphere, and clean it up after centuries of misunderstanding of the Christian mystery.

Christianity fulfills the promise of Judaism. Fulfilling the pattern called Jesus, we are gathered one by one into that one resurrected man, to be that one being in Christ. I don't care what name you bear on earth, you will be sent as Jesus. You will play his part and share your experiences with all who will listen. Do not elaborate; but tell them that unless they believe, it will not happen to them and they will remain in the world of death.

It is not enough to believe only that Christ existed. That is like saying to a friend: "I believe you exist." What an insult! The question is: do you trust Christ? Do you believe in him? Now I - a man - tell you the story of salvation as I have experienced it. Do you believe in my story? If you do, you believe in me; then forget all you hear about me as a man.

A friend recently told an acquaintance the story of my experiences, then later mentioned that I had been divorced and had remarried. The moment the lady heard I was divorced, she closed her mind and could not accept the story that I was called, incorporated into the body of God, and sent to tell. She judged the outer man and could not believe in him whom God has sent. She could go across the street, however, and believe that if she only ate corn she would be saved, because the person who told her so wasn't divorced.

I tell you: you can eat corn from now on, but you will still remain in this world of death until you believe salvation's story as I have experienced it. I don't care what you have done or are doing; if you believe my story and set your hope fully upon that grace which is coming to you, He who sees your belief will call you and erupt within you. God sees your heart. He sees that you are capable of believing the incredible story of Christ and fulfills it.

Ask the doctor who brought you out of your mother's womb to explain how the bones grew there, or how they were covered with flesh; and - although he can give you reasons why they appeared - he cannot tell you how it is done; as we are told in the books of

Ecclesiastes and Proverbs: "Who knows how the bones grow in the womb of woman?

Now I tell you of another birth, which is greater than that which comes out of woman. No one sees this birth, yet it is real, for it is the birth of God. He is born out of this body of death and takes you with him into the body of life. It is not necessary to understand this birth, only to believe in it. So, what must you do to be doing the work of God? Believe in him whom he has sent. And what must you do to be saved? Believe in the Lord Jesus, who is the pattern you have heard about from me. Then go about your business and live fully; enjoy life and all that it has to offer.

A lady recently called, who had heard me many years ago in Detroit and Minneapolis. Although she and her husband had nothing, she believed what I said and imagined having lots of money. Her husband spent many years in different mental hospitals, depleting the little money they had, and then one day he took his own life.

Her only brother was a very thrifty businessman, who lived frugally. He died, and three weeks later his wife died, leaving everything to this lady. Now she has the money to live in luxury, just as she had imagined. This lady assumed wealth without knowing where it would come from, and now she has it.

The law will not fail you here or in the world of God, for you must believe both stories. I tell you: an assumption, though false, if persisted in will prove itself in the world of Caesar, as it did in her case. I also tell you an incredible story: that you will awaken in your skull and experience a spiritual birth as described in scripture; for you are the one spoken of there.

Can you believe both stories? If you believe one enough to test it, and it proves itself in performance, try to believe the other; for unless you believe both, you cannot prove them. If you believe the one in the world of Caesar, you can have money as this lady has. But you must believe the other in order to live where you do not need money, for there you know that the earth is yours and all within it. When you are incorporated into the body of God, you know you are God and everything is yours. Then you will tell your story, depart this world, and return to the Father - who is yourself!

But while you are here, where you do not know the world is all yours, apply the law of assumption. Assume the feeling of the wish fulfilled and let God's law work for you. Learn to believe the story on this level through application, and one day you will believe the incredible story on the higher level.

What must we do to be doing the work of God? Believe in him whom he has sent. Though born of flesh and blood, with four brothers and sisters, and a carpenter by trade, after the second birth he was no longer the man one knew, but an entirely different being. After telling you what happened in him, he asks you to believe it. If you do, you believe in the way you are saved. If you do not, you believe in and will remain in the world of death with its many blows.

Hundreds of millions of people call themselves Christians and believe in the existence of Jesus; but they do not believe in him, for if they did they would believe his story. I have told it in my book, Resurrection. The story is true. I have come to bear witness to it. God incorporated me into his body and sent himself with me, so whoever sees me, sees him who sent me. You will never see the one who sent me by looking at the outer man. It is only the inner man who bears God's likeness, for that is who I am!

Now let us go into the silence.

Believe It In

he objective reality of this world is solely produced by the human imagination, in which all things exist. Tonight, I hope to show you how to subjectively appropriate that which already exists in you, and turn it into an objective fact. Your life is nothing more than the out picturing of your imaginal activity, for your imagination fulfills itself in what your life becomes.

The last year that Robert Frost was with us, he was interviewed by Life Magazine, and said: "Our founding fathers did not believe in the future, they believed it in." This is true. Having broken with England, our founding fathers could have established their own royalty here by making one of them the king, thereby perpetuating a royal family. They could have chosen a form of dictatorship, but they agreed to imagine a form of government that had not been tried since the days of the Greeks. Democracy is the most difficult form of government in the world, yet our founding fathers agreed to believe it in. They knew it would take place, because they knew the power of belief - the power I hope to show you that you are, tonight.

To say: "I am going to be rich," will not make it happen; you must believe riches in by claiming within yourself: "I am rich." You must believe in the present tense, because the active, creative power that you are, is God. He is your awareness, and God alone acts and is. His name forever and ever is "I am" therefore, he can't say: "I will be rich" or "I was rich" but "I am rich!" Claim what you want to be aware of here and now, and - although your reasonable mind denies it and your senses deny it - if you will assume it, with feeling, your inward activity, established and perpetuated, will objectify itself in the outside world - which is nothing more than your imaginal activity, objectified. To attempt to change the circumstances of your life before you change its imaginal activity, is to labor in vain. This I know from experience. I had a friend who hated Roosevelt, yet wanted him to change. Every morning while shaving, my friend would tell Roosevelt off. He found great joy and satisfaction in this daily routine, yet could not understand why Roosevelt stayed the same. But I tell you, if you want someone to change, you must change your imaginal activity, for it is the one and only cause of your life. And you can believe anything in if you will not accept the facts your senses dictate; for nothing is impossible to imagine, and imagining - persisted in and believed - will create its own reality.

Now, all things exist in God, and he exists in you and you exist in him. Your eternal body is the human imagination, and that is God Himself. Your imagination is an actual body in which everything is contained. When you imagine, the thing itself comes out of that divine body, Jehovah. The story of Jesus is a wonderful mystery that cannot be solved until you discover, from experience, that he is your own wonderful human imagination.

We are told that God speaks to man in a dream and unveils himself in a vision. Now, vision is a waking dream like this room, while a dream occurs when you are not fully awake. A few years ago, this vision was mine: I was taken in spirit into one of the early mansions on 5th Avenue in New York City at the turn of the century. As I entered, I saw that three generations were present and I heard the eldest man telling the others of their grandfather's secret. These are his words: "Grandfather used to say, while standing on an empty lot: `I remember when this was an empty lot.' Then he would paint a word picture of what he wanted to build there. He saw it vividly in his mind's eye as he spoke, and in time it was established. He went through life in that manner, objectively realizing what he had first subjectively claimed."

I tell you: everything in your outer world was first subjectively appropriated, I don't care what it is. Desire can be your empty lot where you may stand, remembering when that which you now have, was only a desire. If I now say: "I remember when I lectured at the Woman's Club in Los Angeles" I am implying I am no longer there, and am where I want to be. Remembering when you were poor, I have taken you out of poverty and placed you in comfort. I remember when you were sick, by taking you out of sickness and placing you in the state of health. I remember when you were unknown, implies you are now known. By changing my memory image of you, I can now remember when you, with all your fame and fortune, were unknown and broke. That was the secret of grandfather's success.

This is what I learned in vision. Do not put this thought aside because it came to me in vision. In the 12th chapter of the Book of Numbers it is said that God speaks to man through the medium of dreams and makes himself known through vision. If God makes himself known to you through vision, and speaks to you in dream, what is more important than to remember your dreams and visions? You can't compare the morning's paper or any book you may read, to your vision of the night, for that is an instruction from the depth of yourself.

God in you speaks to you in a dream, as he did to me when he took me on a trip in time to that beautifully staffed mansion at the turn of the century. As spirit, I was invisible to those present; but I heard more distinctly than they, and comprehended the words more graphically then they, because they had their millions; and who is going to tell one who already has millions how to get them. I entered their environment to hear their story, in order to share it with those who will hear and believe my words and then try it.

This doesn't mean that, just because you heard my vision you are going to enjoy wealth; you must apply what you heard, and remember when. If you would say: "I remember when I couldn't afford to spend $400 a month for rent," you are implying you can well afford it now. The words: "I remember when it was a struggle to live on my monthly income," implies you have transcended that limitation. You can put yourself into any state by remembering when. You can remember when your friend expressed her desire to be married. By remembering when she was single, you are persuading yourself that your friend is no longer in that state, as you have moved her from one state into another.

When I say all things exist in the human imagination, I mean infinite states; for everything possible for you to experience now, exists in you as a state of which you are its operant power. Only you can make a state become alive. You must enter a state and animate it in order for it to outpicture itself in your world. You may then go back to sleep and think the objective fact is more real than its subjective state into which you have entered; but may I tell you: all states exist in the imagination. When a state is entered subjectively, it becomes objective in your vegetative world, where it will wax and wane and disappear; but its eternal form will remain forever and can be reanimated and brought back into being through the seed of contemplative thought. So, I tell you: the most creative thing in you is to enter a state, and believe it into being.

Now, causation is the assemblage of mental states, which occurring creates that which the assemblage implies. Let us say that I have two friends who would empathize with me (not sympathize) if they heard my good news. I put them together and listen (all in my imagination) as they talk about me and what has happened in my life. Being true friends, I hear their words of joy and see their happiness reflected on their faces. Then I allow myself to become visible to them and feel their handshake and embrace as I accept their congratulations as a fact. Now I have assembled a mental state, which occurring, created that which the assemblage implied; therefore, I am its cause. As I walk, firmly believing in the reality of what I have done, and that imaginal act becomes a fact, I may question myself as it how it came about. Then, remembering my imaginal act I would say: "I did it." If I did it, then did not God do it? Yes, because God and I are one "I am".

Are you going to continue to believe there is another on the outside; or are you going to believe the great confession of faith, which I would urge you to accept? It's the great Sh'ma: "Hear O Israel, the Lord our God, the Lord is One." If the Lord is one he can't be two; therefore, if his name is I am and you say "l am," you must be one with the Lord who brought the world into being.

Listen to these words: "By faith we understand that the world was created by the word of God, so that things that are seen were made out of things which do not appear." Here we see that the word of God is an imaginal activity, which -joined by faith - created the world. And faith is nothing more than the subjective appropriation of an objective hope. Now, when you discuss your desire with me, you cannot see my imaginal act relative to you. If you tell me you need a job and I accept that thought, when I think of you I remember your need. But if I changed your words and heard you tell me you loved your job, I could remember when you needed one; for now, my memory bank contains the fact that you have a job you like very much. And when we meet again you tell me that you have it, you are only bringing confirmation of my imaginal, creative act.

Now, if imagination works this way, and it proves itself in the testing time and time again, what does it matter what the world thinks? It costs you nothing to try it, and what a change in life it will produce for you. Try it, for you will prove it in performance.

This may be in conflict with what you believe God to be. Maybe you still want him to be someone on the outside, so that there are two of you and not one. That's all right if you do, but I tell you: God became you that there would not be you and God. He became you, that you may become God. If God became you, his name must be in you, and it is; for if I ask you anything, you must first be aware of the question before you can respond, and your awareness is God.

You may not be aware of who you are, where you are, or what you are; but you do know that you are. Aware of what your senses and reason dictate, you may believe that you are limited, unwanted, ignored, and mistreated; and your world confirms your belief in your imaginal activity. And if you do not know that your awareness is causing this mistreatment, you will blame everyone but yourself; yet I tell you the only cause of the phenomena of life is an imaginal activity. There is no other cause.

If you believe in the horrors of the world as they are given to you in the paper and on television, your belief causes the horrors to continue. Believing the news of a shortage, you will buy what you do not need, blindly accepting the pressure to perpetuate an imaginal activity that keeps you frightened. All through scripture you are told to let not your heart be troubled, be not afraid, and fear not. If fear could be eliminated, there would be no need for psychologists or psychiatrists. It's a bunch of nonsense, anyway. Every day this branch of medicine changes their concepts and they are always in conflict as to what a man's attitude towards life is.

I say to everyone: the whole vast world is now in your human imagination, and you can bring any desire out of it by believing it into being.

First, you must know what you want, then create an image that fulfills it. Would your friends know and talk about it? Imagine they are with you now, discussing your fulfilled desire. You could be at a cocktail or dinner party that is being given in your honor. Or maybe it's a little get-together over tea. Create a scene in your mind's eye and believe its reality in! That invisible state will produce the objective state you desire, for all objective reality is solely produced by imagination.

The clothes you are now wearing were first imagined. The chair in which you are seated, the room that surrounds you - there isn't a thing here that wasn't first imagined; so you can see that imagining creates reality. If you don't believe it, you are lost in a world of confusion.

There is no fiction. What is fiction today will be a fact tomorrow. A book written as a fictional story today comes out of the imagination of the one who wrote it, and will become a fact in the tomorrows. If you have a good memory or a good research system, you could find today's facts. Not every fact is recorded, because not every thought is written; yet every person imagines. A man, feeling wrongfully imprisoned and desiring to get even, will disturb the world, because all things by a law divine in one another's being, mingle. You can't stop the force that comes from one who is imagining, because behind the mask he wears, you and he are one. Start now to become aware of what you are thinking, for as you think, you imagine. Only then can you steer a true course to your definite end. If you lose sight of that end, however, you can and will be moved by seeming others. But if you keep your mind centered in the awareness of dwelling in your destination, you cannot fail.

The end of your journey is where your journey begins. When you tell me what you want, do not try to tell me the means necessary to get it, because neither you nor I know them. Just tell me what you want that I may hear you tell me that you have it. If you try to tell me how your desire is going to be fulfilled, I must first rub that thought out before I can replace it with what you want to be. Man insists on talking about his problems. He seems to enjoy recounting them and cannot believe that all he needs to do is state his desire clearly. If you believe that imagination creates reality, you will never allow yourself to dwell on your problems, for you will realize that as you do you perpetuate them all the more.

So, I tell you: the greatest thing you can do is to believe a thing into existence, just as our founding fathers did. They had no current example of democracy. It existed in Greece centuries ago, but failed because the Greeks changed their imaginal activity. We could do that too. Don't think for one second we have to continue as a democracy. We could be under dictatorship within twenty-four hours, for everything is possible. If you like democracy, you must be constantly watchful to keep its concepts alive within you. It's the most difficult form of government. A man can voice an opinion and stage a protest here, but in other forms of government he cannot. If you want to enjoy the freedom of a democracy, you must keep it alive by being aware of it.

Now, if you keep this law, you don't have to broadcast what you want; you simply assume that you have it, for - although your reasonable mind and outer senses deny it - if you persist in your assumption your desire will become your reality. There is no limit to your power of belief, and all things are possible to him who believes. Just imagine what an enormous power that is. You don't have to be nice, good, or wise, for anything is possible to you when you believe that what you are imagining is true. That is the way to success.

I believe any man who has been successful in his life's venture has lived as though he were successful. Living in that state, he can name those who aided him in achieving his success; and he may deny that he was always aware of success, but his awareness compelled the aid he received.

To believe your desire into being is to exercise the wonderful creative power that you are. We are told in the very first Psalm: "Blessed is the man who delights in the law of the Lord. In all that he does, he prospers." This law, as explained in the Sermon on the Mount, is psychological. "You have heard it said of old, thou shalt not commit adultery, but I say unto you, anyone who lusts after a woman has already committed the act of adultery with her in his heart." Here we discover that it is not enough to restrain the impulse on the outside. Adultery is committed the moment the desire is thought!

Knowing what you want, gear yourself towards it, for the act was committed in the wanting. Faith must now be added, for without faith it is impossible to please God. Can you imagine a state and feel that your imaginal act is now a fact? It costs you nothing to imagine; in fact you are imagining every moment in time, but not consciously. But, may I tell you: if you use your creative power by imagining a desire is already fulfilled, when you get it, the circumstances will seem so natural that it will be easy to deny your imagination had anything to do with it, and you could easily believe that it would have happened anyway. But if you do, you will have returned to sleep once again.

First of all, most of us do not even realize our own harvest when it confronts us. And if we do remember that we once imagined it, reason will tell us it would have happened anyway. Reason will remind you that you met a man (seemingly by accident) at a cocktail party who was interested in making money. When he heard your idea, he sent you to see his friend, and look what happened - so really, it would have happened anyway. Then, of course, it is easy to ignore the law, but "Blessed is the man who delights in the law of the Lord. In all that he does he prospers."

Don't forget the law while you are living in the world of Caesar, and apply it wisely; but remember you are not justified by its use. Justification comes through faith. You must have faith in the incredible story that God promised to bring himself out of you, as you! This is God's promise to all, and all are asked to believe it.

It is not what you are, but what you trust God to do, that saves you. And to the degree that you trust God to save you, you will be saved. But he has given us a psychological law to cushion the inevitable blows of life. The law is simple: "As you sow, so shall you reap." It is the law of like begets like. As you imagine, so shall your life become. Knowing what you want, assume the feeling that would be yours if you had it. Persist in that feeling, and in a way, you do not know and could not devise, your desire will become a fact. Grandfather made his fortune by standing on an empty lot and saying to himself: "I remember when this was an empty lot." Then he would paint a beautiful word picture of the structure he desired there. This is a wonderful technique. You can remember when you were unknown, penniless, and ill, or a failure. Remembering when you were, implies you are no longer that, and your power is in its implication.

Use the law and it will take you from success to success, as you conceive success to be. As far as I am concerned, success is to fulfill the promise, and you cannot do that through the law. The promise is fulfilled through faith. Are you holding true to the faith? Examine yourself to see if you are. I have told you an eternal story. Believe it, but do not change it. The story is this: God became you that you may become God. Use the law to cushion the blows while God keeps his promise; and then one day, when your journey is over, you will say: "Into thy hands I commit my spirit. Thou hast redeemed me, O Lord, faithful God." That's the cry on the cross. Commit your spirit to your imaginal act, relax and fall asleep knowing its redemption is assured. Then when you least expect it, God will prove to you that he has redeemed you by awakening in you, as you. Then you will be born, not of blood or of the will of the flesh, or of the will of man, but of God.

Now let us go into the silence.

Biblical Language

"All are Men in Eternity. Rivers, Mountains, Cities, Villages,
All are Human, and when You enter into Their Bosoms,
You walk In Heavens and Earths;
Just as in Your own Bosom You bear Your Heaven And Earth,
and all that You behold, though it appears Without, it is Within,
In Your Imagination of which this World of Mortality is but a Shadow."[1]

ou may ask yourself what Blake is talking about, yet this is the language of the Bible. Biblical language evokes rather than describes. It is telling of another world, another Man and another age; for in truth, all of the places in the Bible are human.

In the Book of Revelation, John sees Jerusalem become a woman, descending out of heaven adorned like a bride for her husband. And in the 5th chapter of Micah we are told that Bethlehem is that woman out of which God comes. Listen to the words carefully: "You, O Bethlehem, are so little to be among the thousands of Judah, yet from you will come forth for me, one who is to rule in Israel, whose origin is from of old, from ancient times. Therefore, he will give them up until that time when she who is in travail has brought forth." Then we read in the 63rd Chapter of Isaiah, "O Lord, thou art our Father, our Redeemer from of old is thy name." Here we see the Ancient of Days as our Father and Redeemer and, like Bethlehem, we are all in travail, redeeming everything and bringing forth the Father of all life as our very self!

One day you will know an imaginative world where the mountains, rivers, cities, and villages are human. Everything will be possible to you there, for when your imaginative faculties awaken, every thought is objectively real. I don't care what it is, your every

---

[1] William Blake's *Jerusalem*, Plate 71:17

33

imaginal act will instantly become an objective fact. This we are told throughout the Old Testament, but its language evokes and man finds it difficult to understand.

In the 14th chapter of Jeremiah you will find these words: "Thou, Lord are in the midst of us. We are called by thy name; leave us not." The Lord's name is "I am." How could anyone exist and have the name "I am" taken from him? If you couldn't say "I am" you would cease to be. You could suffer from total amnesia and not know where you are, who you are, or what you are; but, because God remains faithful to his pledge, you can't stop knowing that you are. And that which is buried in your soul must come forward, and when it does, you are God.

You don't boldly claim, "I am God" without any assurance that you are. That would be silly. To walk the streets proclaiming, "I am God," not having had his plan of salvation unfold within you, would be the height of insanity. But when he reveals himself in you, you don't proclaim it to anyone, you simply know it and live by this knowledge. And the only way he will ever reveal himself in you, as you, is to have his son stand before you and call you "Father." Then, having fulfilled the 89th Psalm, you too will say: "I have found David. He said unto me: 'Thou art my Father, my God, and the Rock of my Salvation.'" When this lad stands before you, you know exactly who he is and who you are, for this relationship was established before that the world was.

Knowing you are the Eternal God who is Father, you will share this fantastic knowledge, not expecting a hundred percent acceptance, but allowing everyone to respond to what you say. Seeing your weaknesses and limitations, some will believe you and some will disbelieve. Don't let it matter to you, simply tell it and go your way until the end of your allotted time. Then, with the discarding of your garment of flesh and blood, your weaknesses are removed and you awaken as God. Those who heard and accepted your experiences will prove your words in the not distant future and they, too, will awaken as the Ancient of Days.

Mortal eyes cannot see the being I really am. I know I am the Ancient of Days. I never began and I will never end. I appear to have begun in time. That is because I buried myself in my creation, in time. I am the Melchizedek of scripture - he who has no father, no mother, no genealogy, no beginning of days, or ending of days. I am eternity, buried in and waking in my creation. And because I am the Father of all life, my son, David - the personification of everything I have given life to, through experience - will stand before me to witness my fatherhood. David's father was called Jesse, which means "I am." It is that father who, recognizing David, says: "Thou art my son, today I have begotten thee."

This experience will be yours when you come out of the fiery furnaces, which each one of us must and will go through. Did the Lord not tell us: "I have tried you in the furnace of affliction (experiences) for my sake; for my own sake I do it, for how should my name be profaned? My glory I will not give to another." There is only God, so he cannot give his glory to another. Having buried himself in his creation, when he rises from his burial place, he is still God, but enhanced beyond measure by reason of becoming his own creation and rising in it, individualized. We are all members of a body which shares in this grand play of rivers, mountains, cities, hills, and villages - all of which are humanity, all men in eternity.

Have you ever reclined in a chair with your eyes closed as in sleep and pictured a stream of water so real you could put your mental hands in it and they are wet? When you cupped your hands and brought them to your mouth, could you feel the water going down your throat? If you have, you know that the state you have entered is very real and personal. That is the power which is in store for you. That is your power tomorrow, when everything will be at your disposal, all based upon your own wonderful human imagination, for that is God.

Taking upon himself all the weaknesses and limitations of the flesh, God became as you are, that you may become as he is. And when he awakens within you, you are he. If you will believe in your own wonderful, imaginative world, everything will be under your control - but everything! And you will know that everyone in your world is within you, to be contacted at will. That no one can escape you; and when you rise within yourself, everyone rises with you. That is the story of scripture.

While you are here you can test your creative power based upon your desires. You may desire something you think you cannot afford, or you don't have the time or the know-how to enjoy it. You can think of a thousand reasons why its possession is impossible; but - hearing that imagination creates reality - you can imagine you have it. But to imagine is not enough; you must have faith enough in your imaginal act to believe in its reality. When you imagine you are the person you want to be, you must firmly believe you already are it; then wait in faith for your assumption to appear in your world, for that imaginal act has its own appointed hour. It will ripen and flower. If it seems long to you - wait, for it is sure and will not be late.

The link between your imaginal act and its fulfillment is your faith, which is nothing more than your subjective appropriation of your objective hope. Hoping your desire - subjectively appropriated - is true, faith is your link to its objectivity. Act as God, and simply let it be so. God said: "Let there be light, Let the sun appear. Let the moon appear." After his imaginal act, God let everything appear, sustaining it by faith, knowing that without faith it is impossible to bring it to pass. "Faith is the assurance of things hoped for, the evidence of things not yet seen." If you have faith in the reality of your imaginal act, it must objectify itself in your world.

Now, in order to really understand scripture, you must have some knowledge of the experiences recorded there, because they are not of this world. The Bible speaks of the New Man who is in you. It is that Man of Spirit that I am appealing to, as he can believe in the reality of an imaginal act. The outer you knows a reality which it can touch, see, and hear. Its belief is based upon the evidence of its five senses and reason. But I am appealing to the Christ in you, who is your own wonderful human imagination, and one with the Lord. This magnificent creative power is buried in you and will rise in you - not as another, but as your very self. This will be done when the wall of perdition, which divides the two of you, is broken down. If I speak of him I am implying the existence of two; but when I say, "I am," I am speaking of only one. So, Christ becomes one with me by becoming my very self. But I will not know that I am he until I have experienced everything scripture tells me only happened to him.

My rebirth is the result of the resurrection of Jesus Christ from the dead, for it is said that he rose from the same grave in which he was buried. Since there is only one skull, only one grave, and I awoke within my skull to discover I am alone, am I not the one who lay down there to sleep? If asked who was having this experience, I would answer, "I am," and "I am" is not two - "I am" is one. I awoke in Golgotha - my own skull - and I came forth from that skull, as it is said that Bethlehem will bring forth someone for me, one who will rule as God.

Try ruling as God! Knowing that all things are possible to your imagination, imagine something that your reason and senses deny, and see if it works. If it does, then did you not rule your world as God? That's how God acts. He imagines and lets it appear. And who is he? The Ancient of Days.

In the Book of Daniel, you are told: "There came one, like a son of man, who was presented to the Ancient of Days and they became one." The word translated "son of man" is the Aramaic for the word "I" or "one." That's all it means. So, when Jesus uses the word, "son of man" he is designating his function as the mediator between the world of man and the kingdom of God. In the Book of John, he says: "O Holy Father, I have made known unto them thy name, the name thou gavest me." Here he tells you the name is "Father," saying, "Holy Father." Now he wants something else. "May the love with which thou hast loved me be in them and I in them," for the Holy Father wears the body of love.

When you step into the presence of the Ancient of Days, you see God in the human form divine, which is infinite love. And when he incorporates you into himself through an embrace, you fuse with love, thereby becoming the Ancient of Days. You know this because you feel it, but love cannot be seen with mortal eyes; and when you tell your story, those who hear you will say: "You? Why you are not yet fifty." In the speaker's case they would say: "You are not yet seventy, yet you know Abraham?" And I would answer, "Before Abraham, was I am." They would then pick up stones to stone me with the facts of life.

Your birth certificate, place of birth, your social, intellectual, and financial backgrounds, are all cataloged, all available as stones to be thrown when you dare to claim that you are known by one who - as a forefather - lived unnumbered centuries ago. One who not only rejoiced to see your day, but saw it and was glad. To claim that you not only know him, but came before him, does not make sense, but is true. That which has no origin, buried itself in that which began in time, in order to raise that which began in time to its own level - which has no origin.

Here we find the story of Nebuchadnezzar and Melchizedek all rolled up into one. Nebuchadnezzar was an insane king - just like Man in this world. And Melchizedek, who has no father or mother, no origin, no beginning or ending in time, is buried within Nebuchadnezzar. Rising in that which began in time, he transforms time into eternity. Here again we have the story of the coming of the Father.

To find the Father of all life is all that is worthwhile. What else is worth finding? To find a million dollars would be wonderful for the moment, but one day the money will be gone, for everything dies here. Even the very heavens are dissolving; but your imagination cannot dissolve, for he is the Father who was before that the world was. So, when imagination rises in you, you are God, even though you are still in a garment which wears out. And when the world calls you dead, it is because you have returned to the Father, as the Father.

As imagination rises in you, you understand the words: "I came out from the Father and I have come into the world. Again, I am leaving the world and returning to the Father." Now the same "I" makes this statement: "Go to my brothers." If we are all brothers, we do not differ from this one "I" in whom the whole thing took place. The gospel is only the record of experiences seen and heard in the soul. So, "Go and tell my brothers I am ascending unto my Father and their Father, to my God and their God." There is no other Father but the one Father, and no other God but the one God, who is in us all as our own wonderful human imagination. When you say, "I am," that's he, and there is no other God.

You will not know you are God, however, until scripture becomes alive and fulfills itself in you. For that purpose and that purpose only did you come into the world. You did not come here to put things right, as the priesthoods would say. This world is a schoolroom, where man is searching for his father; and how long, vast, and severe the anguish before he finds his father, is long to tell. I do not know when God will awaken within you; but I do know that he will, and then you will see the reason behind it all. So, leave the world just as it is and make no attempt to change it.

Every day politicians are trying to change the world. We have many who claim to be our saviors, yet each - like the Hitlers and the Stalins of the world - have clay feet. Still, people will believe in them and you can't stop them, because they are dreaming. Being all imagination, you can't stop man from imagining, and imagining creates reality. Tonight, they are trying to stop cigarette smoking. They tried to stop alcohol back in 1919, and in their doing, those who lived in the gutter became billionaires, making billions that they could not - and did not - declare for taxes. Al Capone made 130 million dollars net a year for fourteen years without paying taxes. They got him for a few thousand on some small infraction - but what happened to the 130 million a year? So, the do-gooders will do it all over again. Now they are going to start banning cigarettes; and instead of receiving six billion dollars in taxes from the industry, the money will go into the hands of those who will see to it that those who want cigarettes get them.

Man, never learns his lesson. I can remember prohibition well. I came to New York City in 1922 and remained there until 1952, so I know New York City well. Old man Rockefeller, the one who really made the fortune, owned about six blocks between 5th and 6th Avenue. His entire family occupied one block on 54th Street. Before Radio City was built, he owned and rented out the two- and three-story buildings there. One day his son said: "Do you realize that all of those buildings are speakeasies?" Here was a Baptist - who gave millions for the dry campaign - renting houses to be used as speakeasies. So, you see, you can blind yourself to anything.

I tell you: prohibition is stupid. You can educate a man out of a state, but you cannot prohibit him from occupying it. If I told you I would give you the earth if you would not think of a monkey for the next 24 hours, I would keep my earth, for you could not do it. Every commandment that is negative will be broken, for "God has consigned all men to disobedience that he may have mercy on all." The moment I give you a command that is negatively worthy, I have consigned you to disobedience. There is only one commandment which is not negative. That one is "Love thy father and mother." Every commandment has to be broken, yet man thinks he is so holy.

A man who recently celebrated his 100th birthday was asked what he thought contributed to his longevity, and he answered, "Smoking! I have been smoking every day of my life since I was eight years old." Another lady, dying of throat cancer at the age of 30, told reporters that she had never smoked a cigarette in her life. My mother never smoked or drank, yet she died a very painful death at the age of 62. My father drank like a fish. He broke every health code. He never read anything concerning what he should eat in order to live, he just lived. He ate what he wanted when he wanted it. He drank what he wanted when he wanted it, and died at 85 from sheer exhaustion. Having these two examples before me, I don't believe in this nonsense relative to what I should eat and drink. I will wear out this body just as I have a suit of clothes, and when I do, men will call me dead; but I will not be dead, I will be one with the Awakened Christ, for I have experienced scripture. David, in the Spirit, called me Father, so now I know my name and will return to that awareness.

Remember, the Bible evokes, it does not describe. There are three kinds of writing: journalism, literature, and scripture. You can study journalism or literature, but not scripture; for it is all revelation, all vision - written to evoke, not describe. As the visions possess you, you will discover that everything in scripture becomes man. The rivers, mountains, cities, villages - all are man.

In the 4th chapter of his book, Daniel shared his vision, saying: "I saw a watcher, a holy one come down from above and heard him say, 'Cut down the tree, cut off its branches, strip its leaves, scatter its fruit, but leave the stump bound in iron and bronze.'" Now the tree becomes a person. "'Water him with the dew of heaven. Take from him the mind of man and let his habitation be among the beasts until seven times pass over him and he learns that the Most High rules the kingdom of men and gives it to whom he will, even to the lowliest among men.' "The tree spoken of here is the tree of life, which grows in the human brain. It has been cut down to the root; but out of that tree of life (called Jesse) will come a shoot, which is what the Father is waiting for. He is waiting for himself to come out of man, individualized as the man he is bringing with him.

So, God - he who created the world and all within it - descended into his creation. And when he rises, in all, he wipes away time and space as we know it, and becomes the only reality.

Now let us go into the silence.

Blake On Religion

hen you are discussing Blake you are discussing one of the greatest spiritual giants of all time. You might just as well discuss St. Paul, for they had the identical visions, the vision of reality. Tonight, we can cover only a portion of his gift to the world. In his "Auguries of Innocence" he says:

> *"To see a World in a Grain of Sand*
> *And a Heaven in a Wild Flower,*
> *Hold Infinity in the palm of your hand*
> *And Eternity in an hour."*

What is the sequence? The most inanimate thing in the world, a grain of sand, and in it to see a world. Then he moves to the first animation, a flower; and then to see harmony, which is Heaven – to see a "Heaven in a Wild Flower." And now he comes to space: "Hold Infinity in the palm of your hand." And then to time: "And Eternity in an hour."

He moves on now to the bird world, to show us the relationship of the whole vast world, the unity of the world, that we are all actively related. That you can't disturb anything at this moment in any way and not actually affect the whole.

> *"A Robin Red breast in a Cage*
> *Puts all Heaven in a Rage."*

We think we can catch the little bird and cage it for our amusement, that which should be set free. He said:

> *"How do you know but ev'ry Bird that cuts the airy way,*
> *Is an immense world of delight, clos'd by your senses five?"*[2]

---

[2] *Marriage of Heaven and Hell*

So, the little

> *"Robin Red breast in a Cage*
> *Puts all Heaven in a Rage.*
> *A dove house fill'd with doves and Pigeons*
> *Shudders Hell thro' all its regions."*

Then he moves on to the next state, in what the world would call evolution, but he doesn't call it that. Now into another aspect of the animal world:

> *"A dog starv'd at his Master's Gate*
> *Predicts the ruin of the State.*
> *A Horse misus'd upon the Road*
> *Calls to Heaven for Human blood."*[3]

And he takes the stages right through. You will read it as you go along.[4] Here is this mental giant who saw the complete relationship of all of us. So, I think I could be isolated were I in a dungeon and I thought of you – my thought is affecting the entire universe. I thought of you with envy, or with hate, or with love, whatever the thought was as I conjured you in my mind's eye and represented to myself as I want you to be, whether it is in hate or in love, I am affecting the whole vast world. And if I believe in the reality of what I have done, it will come to pass. And because we are all one, all interwoven, I will use you without your consent, your knowledge, to fulfill that which I have imagined at that moment.

Then he makes this statement:

> *"What seems to Be, Is, To those to whom*
> *It seems to Be, and is productive of the most dreadful*
> *Consequences to those to whom it seems to be, even of*
> *Torments, Despair, Eternal Death; but the Divine Mercy*
> *Steps beyond and Redeems Man in the Body of Jesus."*[5]

---

[3] *Auguries of Innocence*
[4] *Annotations to Berkeley's Siris* in his *Pickering MS*
[5] *Jerusalem*, Plate 36

He steps beyond. Because of this principle man could be lost forever, not knowing what he is doing, but "Divine Mercy Steps beyond and Redeems Man in the Body of Jesus." "God is Jesus" and we are but members in this divine body, therefore, only one name – we are he. So Blake made this statement: "Man is all Imagination. God is Man and exists in us and we in him."[6]

> *"The Eternal Body of Man is The Imagination,*
> *that is, God himself,*
> *The Divine Body, Jesus;*
> *we are his Members."*[7]

He makes every world, and now he asks us to join with him in putting this to the test. When you read his works from beginning to end, he never waivers from this premise. One thing he asks us all to do and to always bear in mind at every moment in time – to distinguish between the immortal man, which he saw... He said: "When I first did distinguish the immortal man that cannot die. . . that immortal man was Imagination." Imagination has a body and he describes that body when he begs us to always discriminate between this immortal man — your wonderful human Imagination — and the state into which it has fallen.

And so, you may be this night in the state of love (I hope you are), the state of tenderness, the state of affluence. I don't know, but you may not be. You may be in the opposite state. But were you in the opposite state, or some friend of yours, or some total stranger in the opposite state, he begs you, he begs all of us, to always bear in mind the distinction between the occupant of the state and the state, and lift everyone out of the state if it is an unlovely state. For man is like a pilgrim passing through states, as though I pass through the states of this country. If this night I pass through Chicago, Chicago remains, but I — the pilgrim — pass on. If I pass through any state — the state of poverty, when I leave poverty it doesn't really dissolve, it

---

[6] *Annotations to Berkeley's Siris*
[7] *The Laocoön*

hasn't disappeared. I left it for anyone to enter. I hope they will avoid it, but anyone may fall into it or deliberately go into it by feeling sorry for himself, feeling unwanted. And so he tells us of these enormous states, infinite states in the world. That everything possible that could happen to man is already created in the form of states. When man enters the state, the state unfolds because he — the operant power — has entered the state, and unknowingly he simply unfolds the state. If the state is one of wealth, in a way he does not know everyone in the world that can aid the unfolding of that state must aid it. If he enters any state — the state of poverty — though at the moment when he enters it he may have everything in the world, in no time he will grow the fruits of poverty in this world, for he is in the state of poverty. But he, the occupant of the state, is neither rich or poor.

So, Blake calls upon everyone to bear this in mind constantly and forgive every being in the world. For he says: "Mutual forgiveness of each sin, such are the Gates into Heaven in our world." If I could only remember every moment of time when I see someone I dislike, that he is only in a state. That is why I dislike him – I dislike the state. I identify him with the state I dislike, but I think it is the occupant. It is not the occupant. He could come out at any moment in time, or I could get him out if I pulled him out and put him into another state, and I wouldn't dislike him. If I bear this in mind, knowing my power to pull him out of the state I could save him, at least temporarily, until he is actually redeemed by this "Divine Mercy that steps beyond and Redeems Man in the Body of Jesus." And that is a true vision. We are "Redeemed in the Body of Jesus." The day will come when you actually will be pulled into his presence, for it is he, divine mercy, that steps beyond, in spite of what we have done, and pulls us right into his presence.

Then we are asked a very simple question. The world will answer correctly or he would not have told us. It is automatically done — we are divinely prompted what to answer, what to say when the question is asked. We cannot make a mistake, for we are actually prompted from the depths of our soul and we answer. At that very moment he embraces us and we become one with him – Jesus. We are fused into the body of Jesus.

And you say: "Is Jesus a man?" Yes, he is a man. So, Blake makes the statement:

> *"If Thou Humblest Thyself, Thou humblest Me;*
> *Thou also dwell'st in Eternity.*
> *Thou art a Man, God is no more,*
> *Thy own Humanity learn to adore."*[8]

So, when you stand in his presence you are standing in the presence of Man and it is Infinite Man. It is Jesus, and you are actually saved in the body of Jesus, because he embraces you and you are locked in his body, one with his body. You are the body. You aren't locked in the sense that you disappear — you are that being. You become one with Jesus, yet you do not lose your identity. No loss of identity and yet one with God, for God is Jesus. Now this is Blake's teaching and I have proven much of it to my own satisfaction by my own mystical experiences.

Now he comes to discuss the story of the "Virginity of the Virgin." For are we not told in Isaiah 7:14: "Therefore the Lord himself will give you a sign. Behold, a virgin shall conceive and bear a son, and shall call his name Immanuel." The word Immanuel means "God is with us." Listen to it carefully: "She will conceive and bear a son, and call his name Immanuel." The child will be given the name as a token. The child is not the great event; the child will be given a name and is the token of deliverance. The child himself is not the deliverer. The child is simply the sign of an event taking place. Now Blake writes one single little verse and he speaks of it as the "Virginity of the Virgin." You are the virgin, whether you be male or female, I am the virgin, we are all the virgin. I didn't know what was happening to me any more

---

[8] *Everlasting Gospel*

than you will know what is happening to you. He puts it in four little lines:

> *"Whate'er is done to her she cannot know,*
> *And if you'll ask her she will swear it so.*
> *Whether 'tis good or evil none's to blame:*
> *No one can take the pride, no one the shame. "*[9][10]

So, we said in the story: "How can this thing be, seeing that I know not a man?" And through the centuries thousands of columns have been written condemning the act, for it was out of wedlock and they take it on this level. It is not on this level. You are the bride of God, as told us in Isaiah 54:5: "For your Maker is your husband, the Lord of hosts is his name." So, the one who made me is going to sire me, without my knowledge, without my consent. So

> *"Whate'er is done to me I cannot know,*
> *And if you'll ask me I will swear it so*
> *Whether it is good or evil, none's to blame:*
> *No one can take the pride, no one the shame."*

No one can take the pride when I confess openly I gave birth to a child out of wedlock. For no one sired that child and no one can claim he sired it. Now whether it was a shameful thing to perform — well, the world must judge. Whether it be good or evil, well, who knows? But one thing I know: no one can claim they did it, therefore "No one can take the pride, no one the shame" — if it's shame. So, the prophecy was made and he writes in four little lines the story of the "Virginity of the Virgin."

He is telling every being in the world that they are that virgin. And you will be sired by the Holy Spirit, and you will produce in visible form an infant, just as told us in the Gospel. Having produced it you stand amazed because how could you produce it in such an unnatural way? It doesn't happen in a natural way. Therefore, you

---

[9] *Poems from the Note-book*
[10] *On the virginity of the Virgin Mary and Johanna Southcott*

were the virgin who conceived unknowingly, for she said: "How can I conceive, how can I have a child seeing I know not a man?" Then you are told the Holy Spirit will come upon you and the child will be the child of God. But it will only symbolize an event that is taking place, and you will be the son of God. In that act you were the child, who symbolized your acceptance. But the son of God is also God the son, and the son of God is made to say: "I and my Father are one."

Blake saw the whole vision so perfectly, so clearly, and told us in his fabulous works. Said he of the Bible: "I know of no other Christianity and no other Gospel than the liberty both of mind and body to exercise the Divine Arts of Imagination. Imagination the real and eternal world into which we shall all go after the death of this vegetable mortal body." He would accept no other form of Christianity. And he said: "All ritual, all creeds," everything in the form of a ritual "was anti-Christ." No religion means by definition a time, devotion to the most exalted reality that one has experienced. But religion as practiced is simply artifice, creed, ceremony, confession, and all outward show, and Blake would have none of it. The whole thing to him was anti-Christian, because to him the whole thing was from within, something the individual experienced that no one by argument could shake.

Years later, another brilliant mind, William James, made this observation and wrote it in a letter (not in a book) to his son. The son allowed it to be published in 1920 in *The Atlantic Monthly*. In this letter, James said: "The mother seed, the fountain-head of religion, begins in the mystical experience of the individual. All theology, all ecclestiastism, are secondary growth, superimposed. These experiences belong to a region that is deeper, wiser and more practical than that which the intellect inhabits. For this they are indestructible by intellectual arguments and criticism." Blake would have endorsed that one hundred per cent.

You couldn't disturb him. They called him a mad person. Even to this very day they speak of him as one who was unbalanced. He confessed in one of his letters that William Cowper came to him.

Cowper was one of the great poets and himself considered one of the six greatest of all writers of letters in the English tongue. He was a contemporary. He died in 1800, Blake in 1827. He was much older than Blake, and Blake in his letter did not say whether Cowper came to him while he walked this earth or after he made his exit from this earth, because Blake could not conceive of death in any sense of the word — nothing died, all things survived. He said: "Cowper came to me and said to me: 'Would that I were mad always, I cannot rest. Would you not make me truly mad?' Then he said: 'Look at you, you are healthy, and yet you are more mad than all of us. Would that I were as mad. I cannot rest until I am as mad as you are.'" He claimed that was what Cowper said to him. That he would now be a "refugee from unbelief."

We think we are sane when we believe in the evidences of the senses, when we believe in some mathematical state that proves itself in performance. He spoke of Blake as one who was a "real refugee from unbelief." I tell you a fantastic story and you don't believe it. Would that you would believe! Believe it, though reason would deny it and your senses deny it. Just to believe it and become a refugee from unbelief, because true religion cannot be analyzed. You can't rationalize it; it is based upon these mystical experiences in the depths of the soul.

Blake said of the Bible: "The entire Hebrew Bible" . . . he did not mention a few of the works. He didn't mention Ruth, Nehemiah, and things of that sort, but he said: "The Five books of the Decalogue; the books of Joshua and Judges, Samuel, a double book, and Kings, a double book, the Psalms and Prophets, The Four-fold Gospel, and the Revelations everlasting."[11] He did not name the prophets, which he called the latter prophets (also the major): Isaiah, Jeremiah, and Ezekiel. He said these are true vision. He did not mention the Epistles, but he said the four Gospels, Revelation, and the Hebrew Bible are eternal visions of what really exists. He saw it so clearly,

---

[11] *Jerusalem*, Plate 48

that all these characters are personifications of eternal states and communed with these states, for when you commune with them they seem as real as you are. But they are personifications of God's infinite mind; every aspect of his mind is personified. You are not an aspect of the mind, something entirely different. You are one with God. "Man is All Imagination. God is man and exists in us and we in him."[12]

"The Eternal Body of Man is The Imagination, that is God himself; The Divine Body Jesus; we are his Members" — part of the body of Jesus, and because there is only one name, we are he. So we pass through a process, a simple process which you can't evoke, you can't hasten it. But when you least expect it, divine mercy steps beyond and redeems man right into the body of Jesus. Then he passes through these stages, where he is born from above, where suddenly he beholds the divine Son[13] as his son; then the great woven structure of the body, the temple, is torn from top to bottom and he ascends to be one around this infinite throne of Jesus, who is God.

I actually believe it. I can't prove it to you and I can't take you with me into that moment of time where I experienced it. I can only tell you I have experienced it and ask you to believe it and share with me in belief, that you yourself may become a refugee from unbelief. For the man who cannot leave what he can touch with his hands and rationalize, cannot believe. And this is something you are called upon, although you have not seen it. "Blessed is the man who has not seen and still believes." That is how the Gospel of John 20:29 ends. Those who heard about it, who would eventually experience it, like Job (42:5) — he said: "I have heard of thee with the hearing of the ear but now my eye sees thee." He heard about it and then came the experience, and he saw exactly what Blake is talking about, because Blake saw it.

I ask you to believe with me and take his works. I wouldn't attempt to interpret for you. I have so many commentaries of Blake

---

[12] *Annotations to Berkeley's Siris*
[13] *David*

and they cost much more than all of Blake's works put together, any one of them. You can buy Blake for $5.00, all this including his letters. I have invested in Blake's works at home close to a thousand dollars in commentaries, and no two agree as to what Blake means by his fantastic experiences. But I bought all these commentaries of Blake before I had the experience. I could have saved a thousand dollars. I don't regret it. I have them at home and there they stand in my library. Three volumes I paid $100.00 for, published by a dealer just back from England. These are rare volumes. Others he made me pay $55.00 and $65.00 for single volumes. And I have the whole of Blake in a nonesuch volume.

So, you read him and all of a sudden you see exactly what he is trying to tell you, because you had a similar experience. Then comes the unfolding of the flower within you, the tree, and you have the experience, the same thing because all will have the identical experience, colored a little bit differently because we are all unique in God's eye. So, we have the same experience as we unfold on this great tree of life. Just think of it. If I can tell you what I would feel from Blake. Someone said: "He was the last civilized man." Well, I hope not, but that is what was said of him. Blake had no venom in him, no impulse to hurt. He didn't have to restrain the impulse; being all virtuous he acted from impulse and not from rules. He was simply a virtuous man in the sense that he loved people.

If I would take a summary of Blake and tell you what I get out of it, I would say tell your children while they are little tots and teach them: never unnecessarily hurt a creature or desecrate a flower. That is the beginning of reverence, and reverence is the beginning of wisdom. If you couldn't hurt a flower, you couldn't desecrate it. You see little children — not knowing what they are doing but in the presence of adults who should know better — and they will take a lovely rose and tear it and desecrate it. If the parent at that moment (or the adult, whether he is the parent or not) would stop the child and explain not at any time to unnecessarily hurt a creature, take the wings from a butterfly. I did it myself. To take the wings from a fly, to take the wings from something else. No reason for it, but I did it as a child. But I did it when possibly there was no one around like my father or mother to stop me in the act. But I know today from experience: you can take a child in its youth, in its infancy, teach it never unnecessarily to hurt a creature or desecrate a flower. That would be to it the beginning of reverence, and reverence is the beginning of wisdom.

Take George Washington Carver, who would take a flower in his hands and talk to it. The man couldn't hurt it, he was incapable of hurt. He would talk to a sick flower and ask the flower what was wrong with it and try to tell him, that he in turn may bring in the solution to that rose bush — which he did. And he gave us, because he couldn't hurt, this synthetic world of ours. He took the ordinary little peanut. He talked to the peanut and wondered "What are you for why did God make you? He made you for a purpose." And then the peanut communed with George Washington Carver. And today we have 300 by-products from the peanut and hundreds of by-products from the southern pines, and from other things. I heard that gentleman the year he died. Just before he died he spoke in New York City at the forum held every year by the Herald Tribune, always held at the old Waldorf Astoria. He said (and I heard him, I saw him) that: "This concern about tomorrow's not being able to feed the world. From the southern states of this country, forget the northern states, the southern states, we could feed the entire world, and clothe the entire world from the by-products. What we could extract from the southern pine and the peanut and all things, the synthetic world." (He called it "the synthetic world.")

Today you can go into a store and they brag about the synthetic garments. They call it Dacron or some other name and tell you how much better it is than the so-called natural thing that you would normally wear. All these are synthetic garments and they claim they are better in feeling, lasting wear, and everything else. All that goes back to a man who couldn't hurt. And he was born a slave (I think he was sold for a horse or something). So, we have to redeem him. Here was a man born into slavery who couldn't hurt, and he is one of the mental, spiritual giants of the world. If you met him beyond the grave you would see a glorious being like a Blake, because he couldn't hurt.

So I would say to everyone here who is in contact with tomorrow's children: start it. If you start and tell the children never hurt unnecessarily. By that I mean if a horse breaks its foot then you have to destroy it. You can't mend it and the merciful thing to do would be to blow its brains out. That would be a merciful act, but then you would do it not unnecessarily. Blake said:

> *"A Horse misus'd upon the Road*
> *Calls to Heaven for Human blood.*
> *A dog starv'd at his Master's Gate*
> *Predicts the ruin of the State*
> *A Robin Red breast in a Cage*
> *Puts all Heaven in a Rage."*

To take this wonderful thing and cage it for your own amusement when it should cut the airy way. And then he says:

> *"A Skylark wounded in the wing,*
> *A Cherubim does cease to sing."*

You wouldn't think a cherub, one with the seraphim around the throne of God, would — at that very moment when we wound the skylark in its wing — would be silent. But in the inter-related world, all things by a law divine in one another's being mingle. So, you could not wound a skylark in the wing and expect a cherubim to continue to sing. All of a sudden things come to an end by our misuse of this fantastic power that is ours. For being all imagination, as we misuse the power that is imagination we cause cherubim to become silent. We cause the whole of heaven to cry out when we cage something that should be set loose and free in this world.

But you start, and I am quite sure it wouldn't take more than one generation, if the world would believe it, if you start it in the home with children. Take them into the garden and let them see and then watch their reactions. Some may be more violent and tear it off, but stop them right there. Don't hit them, just stop them and explain to them that it is a creation of God — the one who made the stars made this for your enjoyment, not for your destruction — and explain they should not desecrate the flower. Then if you see them taking off the wings of the butterfly, because they are human that way, explain they should never unnecessarily hurt a creature. They would believe it, they trust you, and then suddenly that's part of their structure. They couldn't violate that conditioned mind. Why, it wouldn't take any time to really become a world like a Blake, and what a world that would be!

So, I say to you: Blake, read him. I could talk about him from now to the end of time and never exhaust him. He lived to be seventy years old. He never went to school. His visions began at four, and he thanked his father for not sending him to school to be flogged into memorizing the works of a fool. Even in today's paper, the New York Times, a science editor wrote the story of a man's new concept of the universe – radical departure from what was held last year. Well, this is not final you know. This will be a radical departure from what it will be called next year, and that is man's concept. Whether the thing is really expanding to the limit of complete explosion, or whether it is like a breath — where it will go to a certain point and then once more begin to contract, taking unnumbered trillions of years — they don't know and they hope to find it out through telescopes. So, they are experimenting through the telescope to the mathematical concept. But Blake made this observation:

"God is not a Mathematical Diagram."[14]

---

[14] *Annotations to Berkeley's Siris*

Not in eternity will you find God as a mathematical diagram. When you find him you'll find him as man. So, he said:

"God Appears and God is Light
To those poor Souls who dwell in Night,
But does a Human Form Display
To those who Dwell in Realms of day."[15]

When you meet him, it's man. But how can I describe him when he himself describes the body and the form as love. (How do you describe love? Yet I stood in the presence of love and he was human.) But he said:

"For Mercy has a human heart,
Pity a human face
And Love, the human form divine.[16]

So how are you going to describe love? When I stood in the presence of love it was human and it was Jesus and it is form, but it is infinite love. Then you understand the words concerning forgiveness:

"In Heaven the only Art of Living
Is Forgetting and Forgiving."[17]

And you stand in his presence and you hear these words ring out: "Forgive them; for they know not what they do."[18] "Mutual forgiveness of each vice; such are the Gates of Paradise." No one can get through holding any resentment, because you are holding it against a being when it should be a state, and the states are fixed forever through which we pass.

I would encourage everyone to read Blake. He grows every year bigger and bigger in the minds of men, yet he died and is buried in an unknown grave. I doubt if anyone truly knows where he is buried.

---

[15] *Auguries of Innocence*
[16] *The Divine Image*
[17] *Notes*, Plate 81
[18] *Luke 23:34*

Possibly, because he was poor in those days in England, they buried the paupers four and six to a grave. So, who knows where he is buried? At least we have his works, those that survived. And so, after 200 years here is this giant, and in his day, we had men that can only be remembered because there was certain violence, like George III, who reigned where he lived, when this was a colony. And here this mad George, truly mad, and nothing was more sane than Blake. And George who was then King of England – we founded his colony – could give away sections of it, vast areas to those that he favored – mad as a hatter! And they called Blake the madman! And Cowper, who did go mad (three times he was put away) – he appeared to Blake and asked Blake to make him truly mad. Not mad as the world judges it, because there are unbalanced mental states, no question about it. "Make me as mad, Blake, till I become like you, a refugee from unbelief." He was torn between the two.

If I could only go all out and believe in the reality of my imaginal act and not look back. Just go all out, and believe that things are as I desire them to be. But don't look down now to my understanding to see if it is really happening, like pulling up the little seed to see if it is taking root. Really believe that it is going to take root and in its own way it unfolds within itself and grows. But don't pull it up; walk right out in the belief that things are as I desire them to be, even though at the very moment it seems darker than ever. And if I do that, that is what Blake did.

They said that many a day he had not a potato in the house and no money. His wife must have been an angel of angels. To remind him there was no food in the house – and then he would have to go out and sell one of his paintings, or get a commission to make a painting – she would put before him on the bare table an empty plate and a spoon, so when he came to dinner, well, that's it. He took the hint and then would go out and either borrow a pound or a few shillings, or try to get a commission for a picture he had not yet painted. He lived in that so-called dream world. But what he has done to posterity! How he has affected the entire world. And when you think today that no one who understands the English tongue, called upon to make a list of the six greatest users of English tongue of all times, has the same order of value, but within six they could not omit the name of Blake. And he never went to school. Just that inspired mind, the greatest most wonderful mind.

He said he talked to Isaiah and Ezekiel and he asked them about Imagination and they said: "*In ages of imagination this firm perswasion removed mountains; but many are not capable of a firm perswasion of anything.*"[19]

Well now, I could not if I told you for the rest of my days exhaust or do justice to Blake, but just enough to encourage you to read him for yourself. And take my experience, having paid one thousand dollars for the works of Blake, you buy Blake and omit the commentaries. I have them at home and I read them and they remain read but not to be re-read. But I make Blake my daily companion as I do the Bible. So, take Blake and take the Bible and read it. If you don't understand him at first reading, re-read it and keep on re-reading. I'll tell you one thing it will do for you: it will increase your vocabulary and lift your use of words to the heights.

Now let us go into the silence.

Q & A

Question: What is the symbol of the Lark

Answer: When he said: "A Skylark wounded in the wing, a Cherubim does cease to sing," he identifies that skylark as but the externalized shadow of the song of a cherubim. He calls this the world of shadows[20] faintly reflecting an activity that cannot be seen by mortal eye; that the heavenly world enacted has thrown its shadow to interest man in some strange way in this world. For man is in a world of sea, it is on the sea. His greatest poem, "Jerusalem," begins on the

---

[19] *Marriage of Heaven and Hell*," Plate 12
[20] *Jerusalem*, Plate 71

theme: "Of the Sleep of Ulro!" This fantastic world is called "Ulro" by him, where we are so sound asleep it is likened unto "Eternal Death." And he calls upon us to "Awake." So, all these will aid us to awake. So, if the cherubim by his song in this world, through the shadow of a bird called the "Skylark".

But we go out and we doubt, for instance, as friends of mine (I call them my friends) – wait eagerly for the dove season. And of course, I have always refused their dinner invitations to come and dine on doves. I love the doves. They come all over my place, and when the mourning doves are beginning to coo... And coming from Barbados as I did we have a certain native feeling toward the dove, and so they are fed. If you listen to him carefully the male dove is actually saying: "Moses spoke God's word," and then the female answers: "He did, he did." I listen to it every morning. And then someone shoots him and asks me to come and dine! He tells us of the little lamb: "The Lamb misus'd breeds Public Strife and yet forgives the Butcher's knife." For that purpose, to feed these vegetable bodies — the shadow, the mortal body — you forgive them that use of the knife. But to abuse it: "The Lamb misus'd breeds Public Strife, and yet forgives the Butcher's knife."

Brazen Impudence

new idea will not become part of your common currency of thought until it has been repeated over and over and you begin to live by it.

You have been taught to believe that God exists outside of you, but I say you are all Imagination. That God exists in us and we in him. That our eternal body is the Imagination, and that is God Himself. I mean every word I have just said, but it is a new thought. Until this new idea becomes a part of your thinking, every time you hear the word, "God," your mind will go out to something you have conceived God to be.

When I say I am, I am speaking of the Lord Jesus Christ of the New Testament and the Jehovah of the Old. When you go to bed tonight and put your head on a pillow, you are aware of being. That awareness is God! I want to show you how to use your awareness as brazen impudence.

In the 11th chapter of Luke, it is said that Jesus was praying when one of his disciples said: "Lord, teach us to pray," at which time he gave them the Lord's Prayer. Now, the Lord's Prayer that you and I have is translated from the Latin, which does not have the imperative passive mood necessary to convey the meaning of the prayer. In its original Greek, the prayer is like brazen impudence, for the imperative passive mood is a standing order, something to be done absolutely and continuously. In other words, "Thy will be done," becomes "Thy will must be being done." And "Thy kingdom come" becomes "Thy kingdom must be being restored."

That is not what is being taught, however, as he taught in the form of a parable such as: "Which of you who has a friend would go to him at midnight and say to him, 'Friend, lend me three loaves, for a friend of mine has arrived on a journey and I have nothing to set before him,' and from within he says, 'Do not bother me; the door is shut and my children are in bed. I cannot rise and give you anything.' Yet I tell you, although he will not rise because he is a friend, yet because of his importunity, he will rise and give him whatever he needs." The word importunity means brazen impudence. In other words, he would not take No for an answer!

Jesus was not teaching a disciple on the outside how to pray. He was telling you how to adjust your thinking so you will not take No for an answer. In the story the friend knew what he wanted. He assumed he had it and continued to assume he had it until his assumption took on the feeling of reality and he got it. This is how you find God in yourself, by being persistent in your assumption.

Then this story is told to show how you should pray and not lose heart: "In a certain city there was a judge who neither feared God nor regarded man. There was a widow in that city who came constantly, asking him to vindicate her against her enemies. At first, he refused, then he said to himself, 'Although I neither fear God nor regard man, yet because this woman bothers me I will vindicate her before she wears me out.'" Again, we see the need for persistence in prayer.

When you know how to pray, you will discover that everyone in the world can be used as an instrument to aid the birth of your prayer. They may be condemned in the act and pay society's price, while you are saved; yet you are the cause of their action.

I will now share with you a very personal story. I tell it to illustrate a principle. Society blamed this lady for what she did, and she paid the price, but I was the cause of her misfortune. I am not going to justify my story and if you can't take it, I'm sorry. When I first told it, one lady was very upset and I regret that; but I have noticed that when someone has recently given up alcohol, tobacco, meat, or sex, they invariably condemn the state. They feel too close to it to feel secure. I am not saying that this lady had a similar experience where she was the victim; I am only speaking of a principle. Now here is my story:

When I decided to marry the lady who now bears my name I applied this principle. At the time I was terribly involved. I had married at the age of eighteen and became a father at nineteen. We separated that year, but I never sought a divorce; therefore, my separation was not legal in the state of New York. Sixteen years later, when I fell in love and wanted to marry my present wife, I decided to sleep as though we were married. While sleeping, physically in my hotel room, I slept imaginatively in an apartment, she in one bed and I in the other. My dancing partner did not want me to marry, so she told my wife that I would be seeking a divorce and to make herself scarce - which she did, taking up residence in another state. But I persisted! Night after night I slept in the assumption that I was happily married to the girl I love.

Within a week I received a call requesting me to be in court the next Tuesday morning at 10:00 A.M. Giving me no reason why I should be there, I dismissed the request, thinking it was a hoax played on me by a friend. So, the next Tuesday morning at 9:30 A.M. I was unshaved and only casually dressed, when the phone rang and a lady said: "It would be to your advantage, as a public figure, to be in court this morning, as your wife is on trial." What a shock! I quickly thanked the lady, caught a taxi, and arrived just as court began. My wife had been caught lifting a few items from a store in New York City, which she had not paid for. Asking to speak on her behalf I said: "She is my wife and the mother of my son. Although we have been separated for sixteen years, as far as I know she has never done this before and I do not think she will ever do it again. We have a marvelous son. Please do nothing to her to reflect in any way upon our son, who lives with me. If I may say something, she is eight years my senior and may be passing through a certain emotional state which prompted her to do what she did. If you must sentence her, then please suspend it." The judge then said to me, "In all of my years on the bench I have never heard an appeal like this. Your wife tells me you want a divorce, and here you could have tangible evidence for it, yet you plead for her release." He then sentenced her for six months and suspended the sentence. My wife waited for me at the back of the room and said: "Neville, that was a decent thing to do. Give me the subpoena and I will sign it." We took a taxi together and I did that which was not legal: I served my own subpoena and she signed it.

Now, who was the cause of her misfortune? She lived in another state, but came to New York City to do an act for which she was to be caught and tried. So, I say: every being in the world will serve your purpose, so in the end you will say: "Father forgive them, for they know not what they do." They will move under compulsion to do your will, just as my wife did.

I tell this story only to illustrate a principle. You do not need to ask anyone to aid you in the answer to a prayer, for the simple reason that God is omnipotent and omniscient. He is in you as your own wonderful IAmness. Everyone on the outside is your servant, your slave, ready and able to do your will. All you need do is know what you want. Construct a scene which would imply the fulfillment of your desire. Enter the scene and remain there. If your imaginal counselor (your feeling of fulfillment) agrees with that which is used to illustrate your fulfilled desire, your fantasy will become a fact. If it does not, start all over again by creating a new scene and enter it. It costs you nothing to imagine consciously!

In my own case the scene was a bedroom of an apartment, with my wife in one bed and I in the other, denoting that I was no longer living in a hotel alone. I fell asleep in that state, and within one week I had the necessary papers to start action on a divorce.

This is what the Bible teaches. It is my text book. "Whatever you desire, believe you have already received it and you will!"

There is no limit to the power of belief or to the possibilities of prayer, but you must be brazenly impudent and not take No for an answer. Try it! When I say you are all imagination, I mean it. While standing here on the platform I can, in a split-second, imagine I am standing on the outside, looking at this building. Or, in another second be in London and view the world from there. You say that's all hallucination? That it is all in my imagination? All right, now let me share another experience with you.

I was in New York City when I heard that my seventeen-year-old nephew, my sister's oldest child, was in a terminal state of cancer. I knew how she felt and wondered what I could do to comfort her - to show her that the boy she so loved was not flesh and blood, but spirit. So, while in New York City, I went to my bedroom, closed the door, and lay down on my bed. Knowing that my sister lived in the old family house in Barbados, I assumed I was on the bed where I knew Billy to be. I assumed my sister entered that room but could not see her son, only her brother, Neville. I lost myself in that assumption until my sister, Daphne, entered the room. Looking startled, she came forward, stared at me, then turned and left the room. When I was satisfied that I had seen her, and she had seen me and not her son, I broke the experience and returned to our living room to be with my wife and a friend who had come for cocktails.

Ten days later I received a letter from my sister, in which she said: "Nev, I just can't understand it." Giving the day and the hour, which coincided with mine in New York City, she said: "I went into Billy's room and I was startled to see you there. I knew you were in New York City, yet I could not see Billy on the bed, only you. I must confess I was a bit afraid, so 1 left the room and when I returned I could see Billy again. She could see Billy because by then I had departed. If I am all imagination, I must be where I am in imagination. When I gave the scene sensory vividness, with all the tones of reality, I was seen by my sister two thousand miles away. No, I didn't save Billy. He died, but my presence did convince my sister that her son was not flesh and blood. If her brother, in New York City, could appear to her in Barbados, she knew there was something that inhabits a body which cannot go to eternal death.

I tell you: there is an immortal you that cannot die. That night I gave my sister the conviction of a reality in her son that would survive when the doctor said he was gone. Gone where? Restored to a terrestrial world like this as a young lad, to continue a journey that was set up for him in the beginning. And that is to form the image of

Jesus Christ in him. When that happens, Billy will awaken as Jesus Christ, the one being who is God the Father.

Practice the art of movement. In New York City, my telephone was in the hallway and my chair in the living room. While sitting in my chair, I would assume I was at the telephone. Then I would assume I was looking into the living room. I practiced this exercise. until I discovered I could move anywhere in a split second of time. Try it and perhaps, like my sister, someone will have the strange experience of seeing you where you have not physically been. Make it fun. I do it all the time.

A lady, thinking I was still in Barbados - where she last saw me painfully thin and weighing only 138 pounds - was hoping I was feeling better, when I instantly appeared in her living room. I was brown from the Barbados sun, wearing a gray suit (which I did not own when I left here, but purchased in New York City) when I said: "There is no time," and vanished. Well, she is accustomed to these things, so she was not afraid.

I urge you not to limit yourself to a little body of flesh and blood, for you are spirit. Flesh and blood cannot inherit the kingdom of God, so one day you must take it off. And he who takes it off is immortal. He is your own wonderful human imagination who is God, the Father of all life. When you learn to live this way, life becomes so exciting. Your days are full and you are never alone. I spend all day at home reading the Bible and meditating. I close my eyes and travel the world. It's fun and educational. It expands me and makes me become more aware of the infinite being that I really am.

Now, the two stories from scripture that I have shared with you show the importance of persistence. When you pray, do not get down on your knees and pray to any unknown God. Instead, go to bed and dare to assume you are now who you want to be. Fall asleep assuming it is true and you will be on the road to success, for this is how things are brought into being.

Right now, imagine something lovely for another. They need never know who was the cause of their fortune - but you will. My first wife did not know I was the cause of her action. Had she thought that her act would mean my freedom and her disgrace do you think she would have done it? She moved under compulsion, and I was the compelling force. When you realize this, you forgive everyone for everything they have ever done, because you may have been the one who was the cause of their action.

Blake said: "Why stand we here trembling around calling on God for help and not ourselves in whom God dwells." Why call on any god, when the only God dwells within you? He is not pretending, but actually became you. When you confine yourself to the little garment you wear, you are confining God, because it is he who is wearing it.

You need no intermediary between you and yourself, who is God. Don't run from this city to another in the hope of finding something better, because the one person you are going to take with you is yourself; so, resolve your problems here. Do not compromise. Decide exactly what you want and assume you have it. If your world would change, determine what it would look like; then construct a scene which would imply you are there. If your mental construction comes close to your fulfilled desire, your little day dream will become a fact! And when it does, will it matter what others think about your principle? Having proved itself in performance, share your experience with another that they may share theirs. Keep sharing this principle, because in the end we are all the one being who is the Lord Jesus Christ. One body, one Lord, one Spirit, one God and Father of all. Don't be ashamed to claim it. Man sees the Lord Jesus Christ as some little being on the outside; but he is in you, and when you see him, he will look just like you!

A friend recently shared this sweet vision with me. She said: "I saw a man in a white robe standing on a hill, building a canopy over the entrance to a temple. As I approached I could see that the stripes used for the canopy were translucent green and I remarked how radiantly beautiful they were. The man turned to look at me and I realized it was you, Neville, and yet you were Michelangelo. Then you addressed me saying: 'I have been working on this throughout eternity and it still remains invisible to others'. Taking the stripes, I wove them into the form of a basket and you thanked me and said: 'Great work' and I awoke." That was a beautiful dream. I have been telling the story of the resurrection throughout eternity, but it has never been put into living form. It still remains dead, like Michelangelo's Pieta, or his David made out of marble.

Let David become alive in the minds of others. Give life to the Pieta, the crucified one on the mother's lap. The story is public property, now a dead written code awaiting life in the imagination of men. Dramatize salvation's story. Make it into a play or a television show and let Michelangelo's Pieta become alive. I have made the story alive because I have experienced it.

Michelangelo, with his tremendous know-how of the human form, created the dead forms made of marble. I came along, unable to mold a stick, to find the dead forms taking on life in me. It is my hope that one day this wonderful story will be told as it really is, against the story that we have heard for over two thousand years.

Now let us go into the silence.

Building Your Temple

illiam Blake, in his poem "The Four Zoas: A Dream of Nine Nights," tells of God's fall into division and his resurrection to unity - his fall into generation, decay, and death and his resurrection into the unity of the one Father. Associating his poem with the 6th chapter of Ephesians, the 12th verse, he states: "We wrestle not with flesh and blood, but against principalities, against powers, against the rulers of the darkness of this world, against spiritual wickedness in heavenly places." So, we see that the fall into division and the resurrection into unity is mental.

From beginning to end, the Bible speaks of a certain temple that is being constructed. And every day we are building our temple for the dwelling place of God the Father. In the 2nd chapter of the Book of Ephesians, we are told: "The whole structure is joined together and grows into a holy temple in the Lord; in whom you also are built into it as a living structure of God in the Spirit." In other words, as you bring your building and I bring mine, we are fitted together as living stones in the building of God.

Let me explain this with a story told me just this past week. This is an experience of a lady who is very much a lady and only recently had a little baby. She said: "In my dream I am three people. I am myself, yet I am a man. As myself, I long for a little green dog. Becoming another, I see my dog standing among others. He shines like the sun and because I have ordered him I know all I have to do is wait for his arrival.

"Now, in my dream I am always the sender. When something is to be told, I tell it to another (which is myself), then I become the other in order to retell the story to the third. Becoming the third, I then tell the second to tell the first. I know it doesn't make sense on this level, but as the third person speaking, I hear the message as the second, and say to myself - the first: 'The dog is yours now.' And as the first I am so happy to hear the news.

"Again, as the third person, I tell the second to say to the first: 'Your building is finished. All you have to do is turn around to take it.' Now as the first person, my little dog disappears and I am looking at my many new buildings being constructed. Then I remember that my building is finished and all I have to do is turn around and claim it - when my little baby cries and awakens me."

On the surface her vision appears to be nothing, but it has tremendous significance. Her green dog shining like the sun is Caleb in scripture. Caleb is he who goes with Joshua into the Promised Land. In the story, Caleb - having faith in the God who promised Israel land - was sent by Moses along with other spies into Canaan. Upon returning, Caleb said: "Attack immediately" but the men who had gone with him were afraid; so only the two, Caleb and Joshua (the Hebraic form of the word "Jesus"), entered.

In her dream she is waiting for a little green dog. The word "green" in this dream means "pressing with sap; luscious; health." Bursting with all that is mine, I will take you to lie down in green pastures. Full of faith in the God who promised land to Israel, Caleb is highly recommended, as only two can enter. Others had the dog and others will find him, for she is not the only one who enters the promised land. Now, who was waiting for his companion? God! As the third, the second is told and tells the first that the dog is now hers. Then the experience is repeated, as she once more becomes the sender (the teller), but she is never the receiver, for God only acts and is in existing beings or men.

Now, as the first person she realizes that the little dog has disappeared. Why? Because she has already entered the promised land. Seeing the fabulous construction going on, she is reminded that her building is finished and all she had to do is turn around and see it. There are two passages in scripture, one in the 12th chapter of Acts and the other in the 15th chapter of Luke, where the Greek word "heautou" is translated "he came to himself." In the Book of Luke these words were spoken of the prodigal son. And in the Book of Acts, Peter was imprisoned and shackled in chains. His garments were sold and he was alone in the cell, when the angel of the Lord entered, touched him, and as he rose, it is said: "he came to himself." Now, this word "heautou" could have been translated, "he turned around; it is fulfilled; it is finished; to be married." And she heard the words: "All you need to do is turn around." Turn around and you will behold the finished structure. As a living stone you have now contributed to the overall structure, which is the temple of the Living God. I know from my own experience, everyone contributes to that one Living Stone called the kingdom of heaven! You will be turned around by a force that is greater than anything known to man, but it will not happen until the end. You cannot physically turn around, nor can you force the mind to do it.

Now, Blake tells us: "God fell into division" and this lady divided herself into three. Now heading for the end of the journey, when the force that is holding you to this world is relieved, you will turn around to see the structure your Father built and you will know that you are He. Your temple is not built by another. "He who began a good work in you will bring it to completion at the day of Jesus Christ." Who is he? I am he who began the good work in you. "I have tried you in the furnaces of affliction. For my own sake I do it, for my own sake, for how should my name be profaned? My glory I will not give to another." Your journey is at its end, my dear. You saw the perfect vision. Your building is finished and all you have to do is turn around. This will come at the end, for if you should turn around you will vanish, for, like Paul, you have fought the good fight. Let no one tell you Paul was exaggerating; it is a fight, for we are contending not with flesh and blood.

At the present moment someone is treading the wine press of hate, and - unrestrained - the thought is sent on its wings of feeling. Perhaps sitting in a dungeon this night, someone is treading the wine press of war, and some little boy out in the field catches the idea and wanting to be a hero dreams of becoming a great general, commanding the destruction of the world. He is dreaming and you can't stop his dream. So you are not warring against flesh and blood, but against principalities, against powers and spiritual wickedness in heavenly places, and heaven is within. In the inside of your mind these abominable, loathsome beings are carved. They are unseen forces impinging upon you morning, noon, and night.

But oh, what a thrill to get a letter of this nature! Her building is finished. She now knows that she only sends! She gave the order, saw herself as another, receiving, but when the message must be retold she once more became the teller. And when it is to be experienced, she will be the one who experiences it. So God only acts and is in existing beings or men, for God is playing all the parts.

In the end everyone brings his living temple to the house of God. Ephesians tells us how the structure is joined together and how the holy temple grows in the Spirit. It's a spiritual temple, not one in this world. Scripture calls the church "the body of Christ", but the word translated "church" is "communion of the assemblage of the redeemed." It's the assemblage of those whose building is finished. Playing the part of the receiver, we are the one being who is the builder. Finding Caleb, you (as Joshua, who is Jesus) are led into the Promised Land, as scripture is fulfilled. Having shone like the sun in order to lead you in, Caleb disappears leaving Jesus only. And who is Jesus? Your own wonderful human imagination!

Now let me share another story. Three years ago, in a dream, this lady saw a man who embodied everything she could ever desire. They fell in love and an engagement was announced. Then, thinking she was awake, she put on her nightgown and retired in the hope that he would join her. But as he entered the room the man shook his head and said: "Not yet, but I will return." This month the same man returned and implied by his look that he had come to complete the promise of marriage. I can tell her that, although it hasn't been accomplished, she had the perfect revelation of that which is coming to her. She now has the assurance that: "I will come again and receive you into myself, that where I am there, you shall be also." This is all beautiful symbolism. This lady is not about to be married in this world of ours to a flesh and blood man of such magnitude. No, he is the symbol of the being spoken of in Isaiah: "Your maker is your husband, the Lord of Hosts is his name." The promise is being kept in her. and one day she will turn around within herself and become that living temple of the Risen Lord.

I have seen the temple, and when I leave the garment relative to this age I will enter an entirely different age. And like Paul it is my desire to depart and be with Christ, but it is more important at the moment to remain and encourage you, even though you are fighting against principalities, powers of darkness, and all the horrors of the world. But I have seen the building being constructed for you, not by another, but by your deeper self, who is God the Father.

In 1952, while living in New York City, I had a thirst that only an experience of God could quench. "As the hart panteth after the waterways, so panteth my soul after thee, Oh God." Then one night out of the blue I found myself fulfilling the 42nd Psalm: "These things I remember, as I pour out my soul. How I went with the throng and led them in procession to the house of God."

That night I found myself leading an enormous procession toward the house of God. It was still in the distance, but as I led them a voice rang out: "And God walks with them." A woman at my side questioned the voice, saying: "If God walks with us, where is he?" And the voice replied: "At your side." Looking at me and seeing a man of flesh and blood, she said: "You mean Neville is God?" and the voice replied: "Yes, in the act of waking." Then the voice spoke only to me, saying: "I laid myself down within you to sleep and as I slept I dreamed a dream. I dreamed..." and suddenly I knew that he was dreaming he was me. At that moment memory returned, and I became six vortices, which I felt enter my hands, my feet, my head, and my side. That was when I knew the ecstasy of the crucifixion.

Paul, in his letter to the Romans, divided the tenses, saying: "If we have been united with him in a death like his, we shall certainly be united with him in a resurrection like his." The crucifixion is past.

"He chose us in him before the foundation of the world." If this is true, then the universal Christ gave us himself, for did he not say: "No man takes my life, I lay it down myself. I have the power to lay it down and the power to lift it up again." And we are laid down with him, because he chose us in him before the foundation of the world. So, if you are united with him in a death like his, you will certainly be united with him in a resurrection like his. I know this is true, for he was resurrected in me, confirming the story of scripture. This is how the structure is enhanced and grows in God. And when the final curtain comes down and the temple is perfect, you will be God the Father and I will be God the Father, yet none of us will lose our identity!

Now I ask you to continue to test your creative power by practicing revision. If you hear something that is unlovely, don't accept it, but instantly revise it. Hear the words that ought to have been spoken and persuade yourself, to the best of your ability, that it is so. What would it matter if you owned the world tonight and departed tomorrow to find yourself working as a fry cook, serving up flap cakes? Live your life fully while here, but remember you can't take your money with you.

So, enjoy the things of this world and apply this wonderful law for yourself and others, for imagining truly does create reality. And remember: you are not wrestling against flesh and blood, but against principalities and powers and darkness of the rulers of this world and spiritual evil in heavenly places. And one day, you who have fallen into division will resurrect into unity!

Now let us go into the silence.

www.ingramcontent.com/pod-product-compliance
Lightning Source LLC
Chambersburg PA
CBHW020603030426
42337CB00013B/1193